# Painting with God

Painting With God

Copyright © 2012 by Charlene Mueller



Photographer: Johnston Photography, Crystal Lake, IL
Editing: Gail Anne Rover

ISBN: 978-1-60920-039-8

Ajoyin Publishing, Inc.
P.O. 342
Three Rivers, MI 49093
www.ajoyin.com



Please direct your inquiries to admin@ajoyin.com

Author may be contacted at PaintingwithGod@muellernetwork.com

# 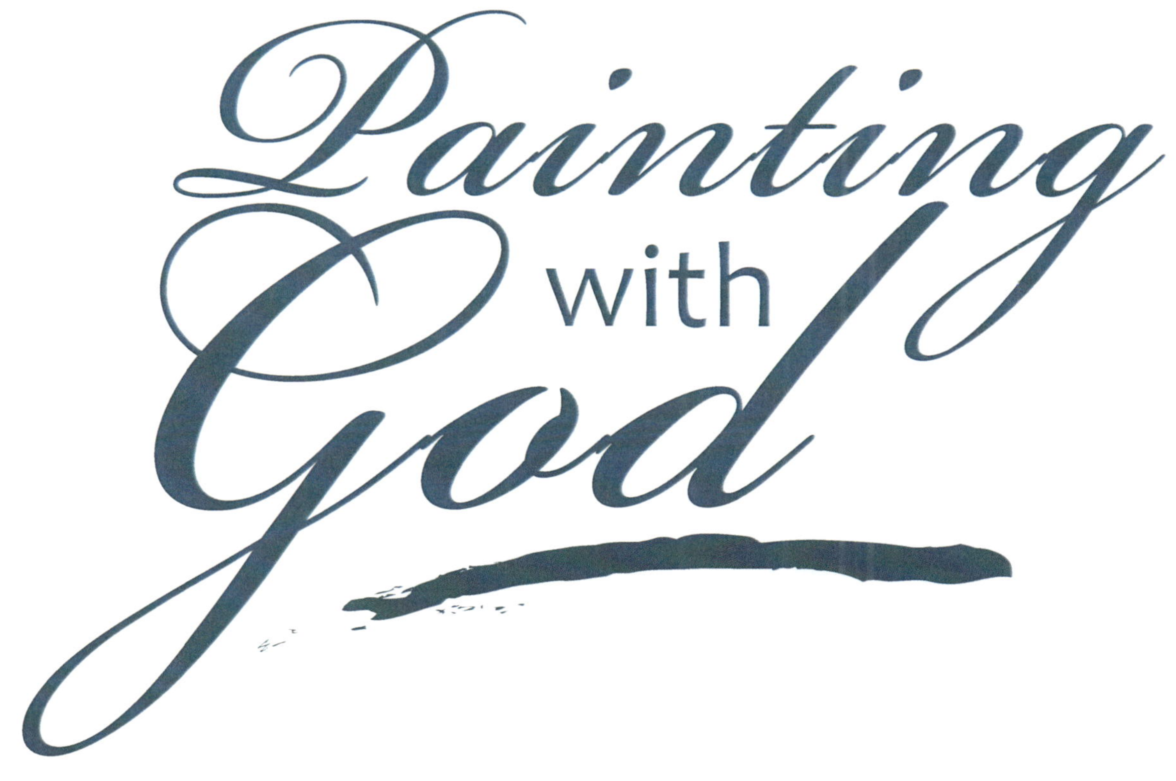 Painting with God

Charlene Mueller

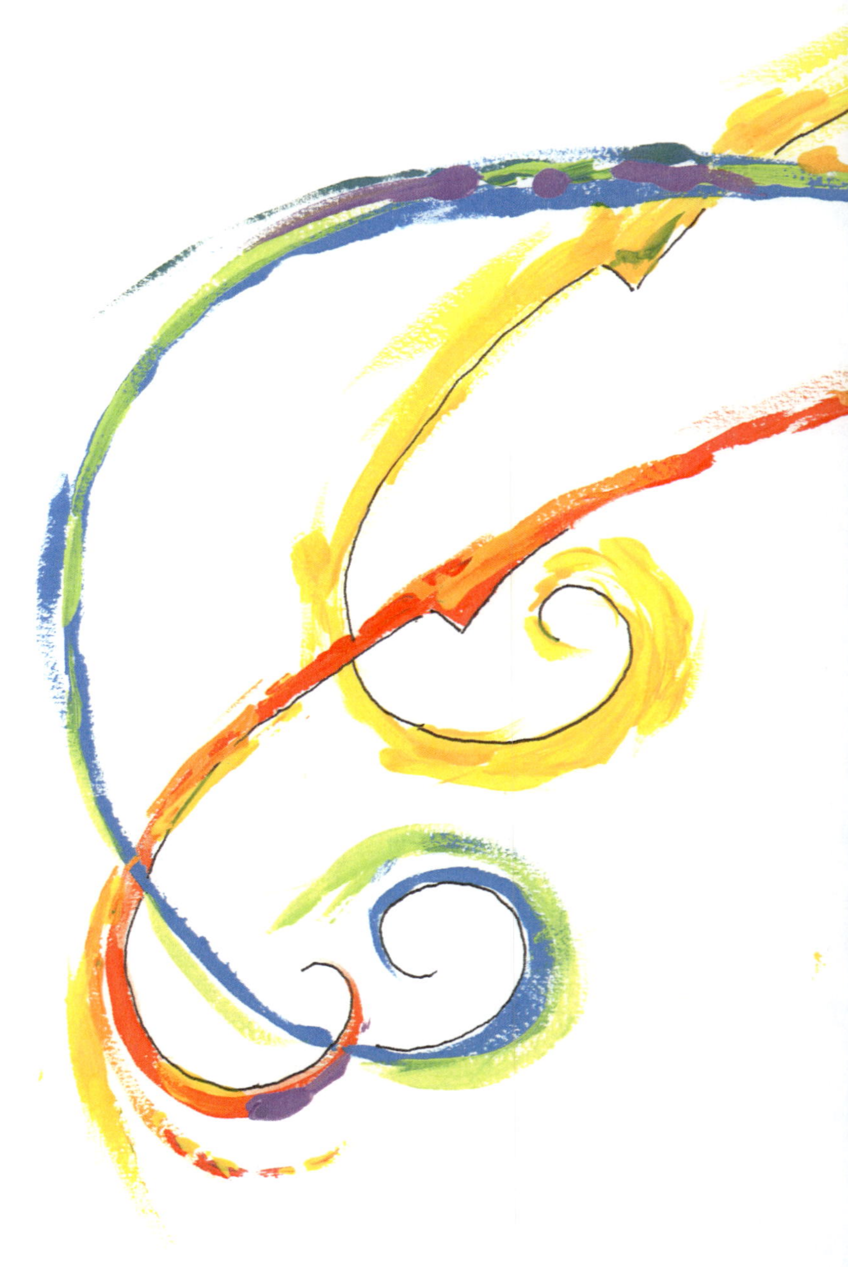

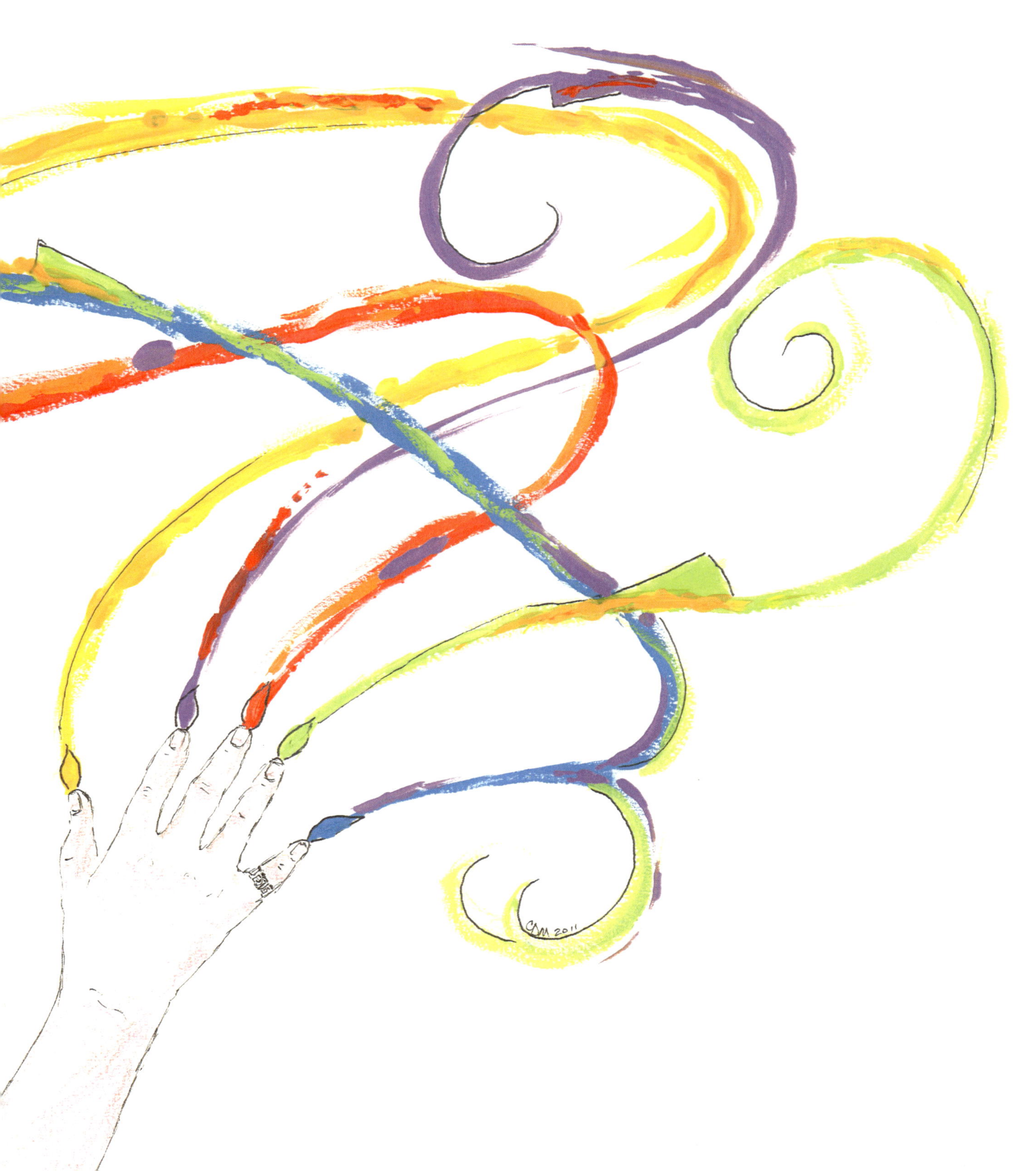

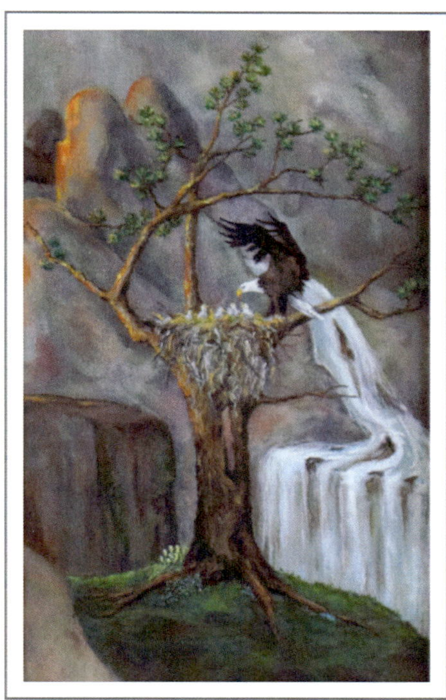

*"Charlene's paintings are stunning and vivid. Each composition tells a unique story that gives us one sliver, a tiny glimpse at our big and wonderful God. Textures, colors, and dynamic strokes all add to the emotional weight of each piece, from dark, heavy themes to bright and imaginative scenes. Charlene has humbly stewarded the gifts the Lord has given her and this art truly reflects His glory."*

—Randy Warren, Filmmaker, Nuru International

*"This artist uses her paintings to reel in inquisitive fish. Let yourself get caught up in the artwork and inspiring words."*

—Sharon Hein
  Language Arts teacher

*"Charlene speaks from her heart. She is a visionary—she senses something within her and is able to put it down on both canvas and paper. Her work is both an expression and extension of her body, soul, and spirit."*

—Mike Hein, Pastor

*"Charlene does a masterful job of marrying her life giving stories with the beautiful paintings the Lord has given her. These stories and parables obviously come from her close and childlike relationship with the Lord bringing insight, revelation and God's love to the reader."*

—Lois Koss is co-founder of Tree of Ministries International, Church–Aglow Regional Coordinator and
  Transformation Team Leader for Aglow Ministries.

*"Serenity' is what comes to mind upon reading the many wonderful stories that Charlene writes. A knowing that God is in absolute control is the common thread woven throughout her works. The Lord has truly blessed her with many gifts that shine through her brilliant use of paint and amazing flare with pen. I have been blessed in years past by the most beautiful paintings that capture such anointed visions and now to read the stories behind each painting is an incredible blessing."*

—Laura A. Shallcross, B.A.
    High School Spanish/Art teacher
    Personal Trainer/Fitness consultant
    Freelance artist
    Gospel/Inspirational singer

*"When Charlene paints, she paints the journal in her heart and reaches hearts. She imparts her proven faith through each visual experience to enrich our own pilgrimage. Charlene know Jesus in a spectrum of friendship and trust that few can express so well. He is real and available to her—and to us! In need or in joy, our knowledge of Jesus is richly amplified by Charlene's paintings. He strengthens and expands our faith through Charlene's art.*

—Dr. Georganne Schweickert
    Founder of Knowing Him Ministries, International
    Ordained in 2004
    IFOC Chaplain; CERT, CISM, and FEMA certified for disaster relief
    Ministered in seven overseas countries and nine states
    Member of White Horse Christian Center and FIM apostolic networks

*"The light of Jesus is reflected in Ms. Mueller's paintings. One can experience Him by gazing at her paintings. My children enjoy the array of colors and are drawn to the Spirit."*

—Donald C. Stinespring, Jr.
    Men's Ministry Leader
    Vision Team Member of Maranatha Assembly of God
    Attorney and Member of Alliance Defense Fund

*"I have been moved and challenged by Charlene's paintings and stories as parables of Truth. They cause me to see in 3D what we often see in one dimension from words on a page…they bring out the depth of what we already know I our hearts by God's Spirit I have related to my sister in Jesus in local church and small group activities over the years I appreciate her gifts and I like her painting of the ship on the sea…that is displayed in her local church." (Painting: A Call to Purpose)*

—Tim Koss
    Global Media Outreach/Response Center Ementor

To my friend
Jean...

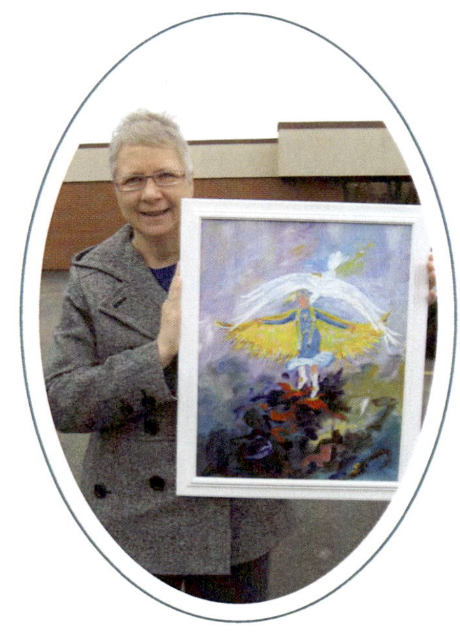

She dances on

wings of prayer.

# Table of Contents

# Remembering

Jesus, I searched for you
as a little child lost.
Now I know
You were always there.
Waiting.
I am lifted up,
safe in Your arms.
You smile.
No matter my age,
forever and always,
Your little girl.

You said to me,
"Empty your heart into My lap,
let Me examine the contents.
Together we will clean, repair, and
restore order.
Say to Me,
I choose You!
I say to you,
What would be your heart's desire?"

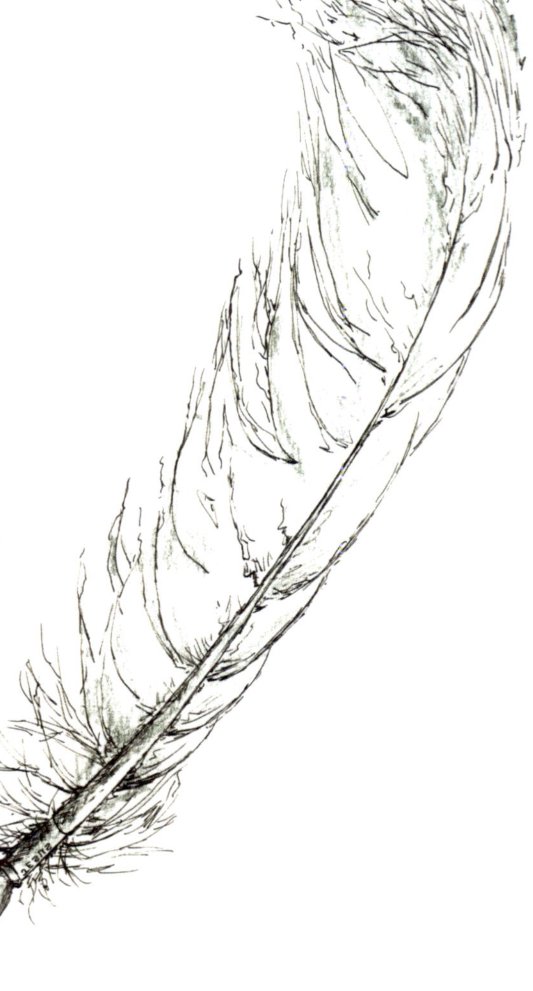

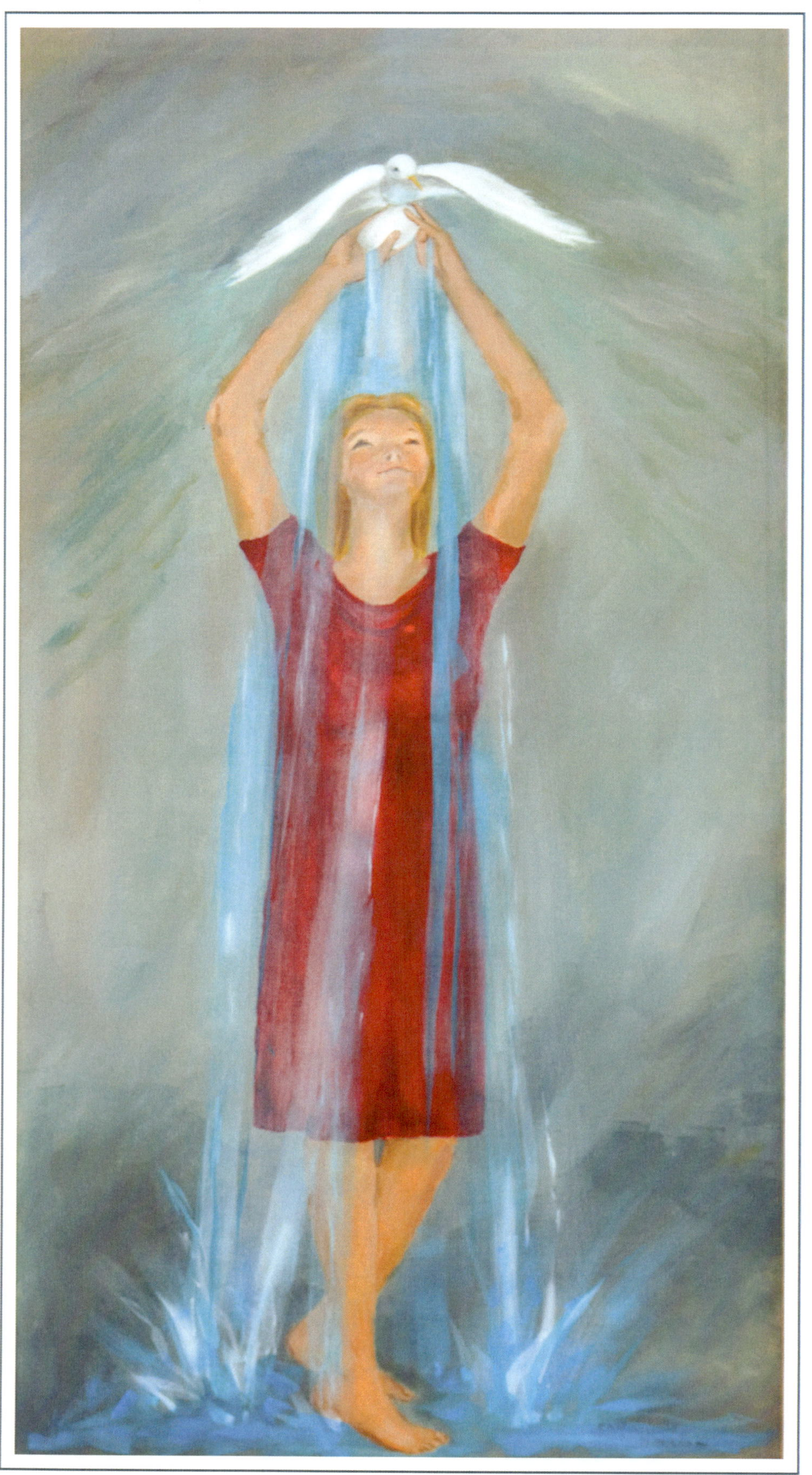

# The Forgiveness Soap

## The Painting

The young girl reaches up; she holds in her hands a bar of soap. Above her, a snow-white dove hovers, then lands lightly on the soap. Water begins to flow over her in streams; she stands barefoot in a splashing pool of blue. The dove and the water portray symbols of the Holy Spirit. Her face reflects her joy in being clean again; she glories in the washing of God's forgiving love. This is the second rendering, painted on a large canvas; come, let me tell you the remarkable way the original painting came to be ….

## The Story

Buttery crumbs and an empty coffee mug were all that was left of my morning's breakfast with Jesus. I liked to wake up early, while my family slept; it was a private time to read my Bible, pray, and journal. I was sitting, hands cupped upward in my lap, feeling very content.

Then something amazing happened. I distinctly saw and felt a bar of soap drop into my hands—just for a half-second—and then it was gone. I sat straight up and I heard these words: "Jesus gives each new Christian a hard-milled bar of forgiveness soap that can never wash away." I literally grabbed my journal and wrote, as my mind filled with questions. Then I sat very still, listening, but no more thoughts came.

Later that day, a picture of a girl entered my mind. As I sketched this in my journal, answers to my earlier questions came as well:

"What am I to do with this bar of forgiveness soap?"

"When forgiveness is needed, talk to Jesus. Tell Him about the ache in your heart, and the sin. Then, when your heart is in step with His, lift your arms over your head, holding the forgiveness soap. Lather the soap with Living Water—the Holy Spirit—and let the bubbles flow down, cascading as a bridal veil."

"How often may I come to Him?"

"Seventy times seven—He does not keep count."

"What am I to do with this sketch and the images You have given me?"

"Hear ye, hear ye, now paint this!"

I had to chuckle. I knew more instructions would be coming. It was a month later, during prayer, I was given two scriptures, which I added to my journal:

> "But who can endure the day of His coming? And who can stand when He appears? For He is like a refiner's fire and like fullers' soap" (Malachi 3:2).

> "If we confess our sins, He is faithful and righteous to forgive us our sins and to cleanse us from all unrighteousness" (1 John 1:9).

I began my preparations to paint, but first I had one more burning question: "What am I to do with the painting?"

The answer came quickly: "Send it to Ed."

Ed? Then I remembered, Ed the farmer.

I chose a small wooden plaque instead of a canvas, and, using garish colors, I painted a girl with bleach-blond hair wearing a gaudy, red dress. Her face was heavily made-up; she was coarse looking. As I painted, the bubbles that flowed down from the forgiveness soap became a lovely bridal headdress and a flowing veil, softening and transforming her.

This is the painting God had me send to Ed (not his real name), a big, soft-spoken man who wears bib overalls and looks like a kindly father. Ed had a ministry that started one day in a most unusual way. While driving into St. Louis, his route took him through the "red-light" district, the area where prostitutes worked the streets. Passing a young girl standing alone on a corner, he felt especially sad about her situation. Then he heard: "Stop! Go back and pick that girl up, give her a ten dollar bill, and tell her of *Me*."

Ed kept driving, thinking, "No, that can't be God." When he heard the same words again, he pulled over and prayed, "Is that You, Jesus?" Ed soon realized it was. He turned the car around, picked up the girl, and spent the next hour telling her of Jesus. This was the beginning. Little by little, a trust developed between the farmer and the many other girls and women caught up in their seemingly no-way-out position. Sometimes he let them sleep in the backseat of his car as he drove the streets, because the pimps would not let them sleep until they had worked their quota of tricks. When their little ones were sick, the women brought them to Ed for prayer. He listened to their stories, and offered encouragement, like a father.

He and his wife turned their farmhouse into a halfway station. There on that farm, Jesus entered into the tangled night of the women's souls and set them free. As for my little painting, Ed took to carrying it with him as he traveled the streets with Jesus, looking—always looking—for the lost ones. The women would come and sit in his car, and he never tired of telling them the story of the cross. I can imagine them holding the painting, sliding their fingers down the veil and thinking, "Can Jesus really wash me clean?" For some, it was the first time they had heard any words of forgiveness.

The pimps hated Ed. One day, as he sat talking with someone in his car, a hand with a gun reached in the window … and fired.

I have heard Ed tell about this extraordinary experience. He said he felt the presence of Jesus surround him—then he saw Jesus smile. The bullet never touched him. Two days later, however, fear did; he was scared, and his strong sense of Jesus was gone. Ed eventually learned to rebuke this fear. He has had to do this many times over. As the ministry continued Ed discovered, as we must, that Jesus will meet us in unexpected ways when we are in need of protection, but as in the everyday walk with a friend, sometimes there is silence.

~ ~ ~ ~ ~

I have been chastised for this painting, a wagging finger shoved into my face, as its owner rants, "There is no such thing as forgiveness soap!" After thinking about this, I have come to a conclusion. Sin clings to us as we walk in this world—through the evil we experience, the evil we see, and the evil we hear. When I remembered how Jesus washed His disciples' feet, I decided to keep my bar of "forgiveness soap" close.

*Happy lathering to you!*

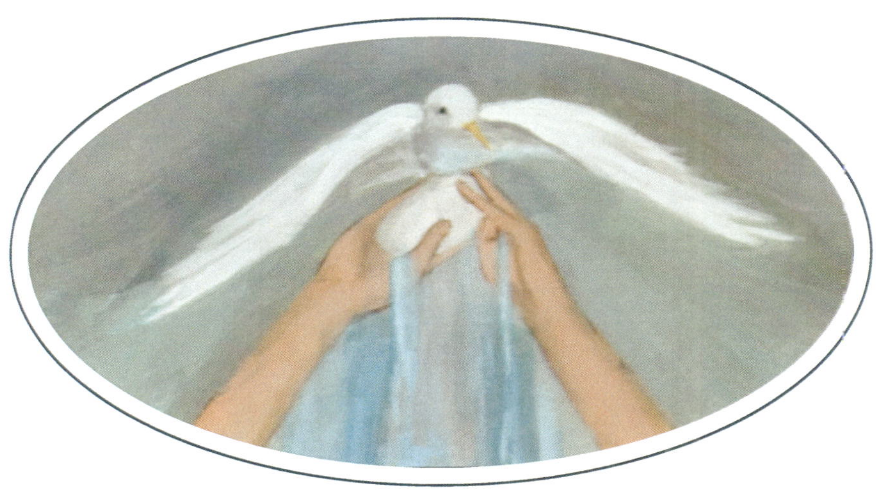

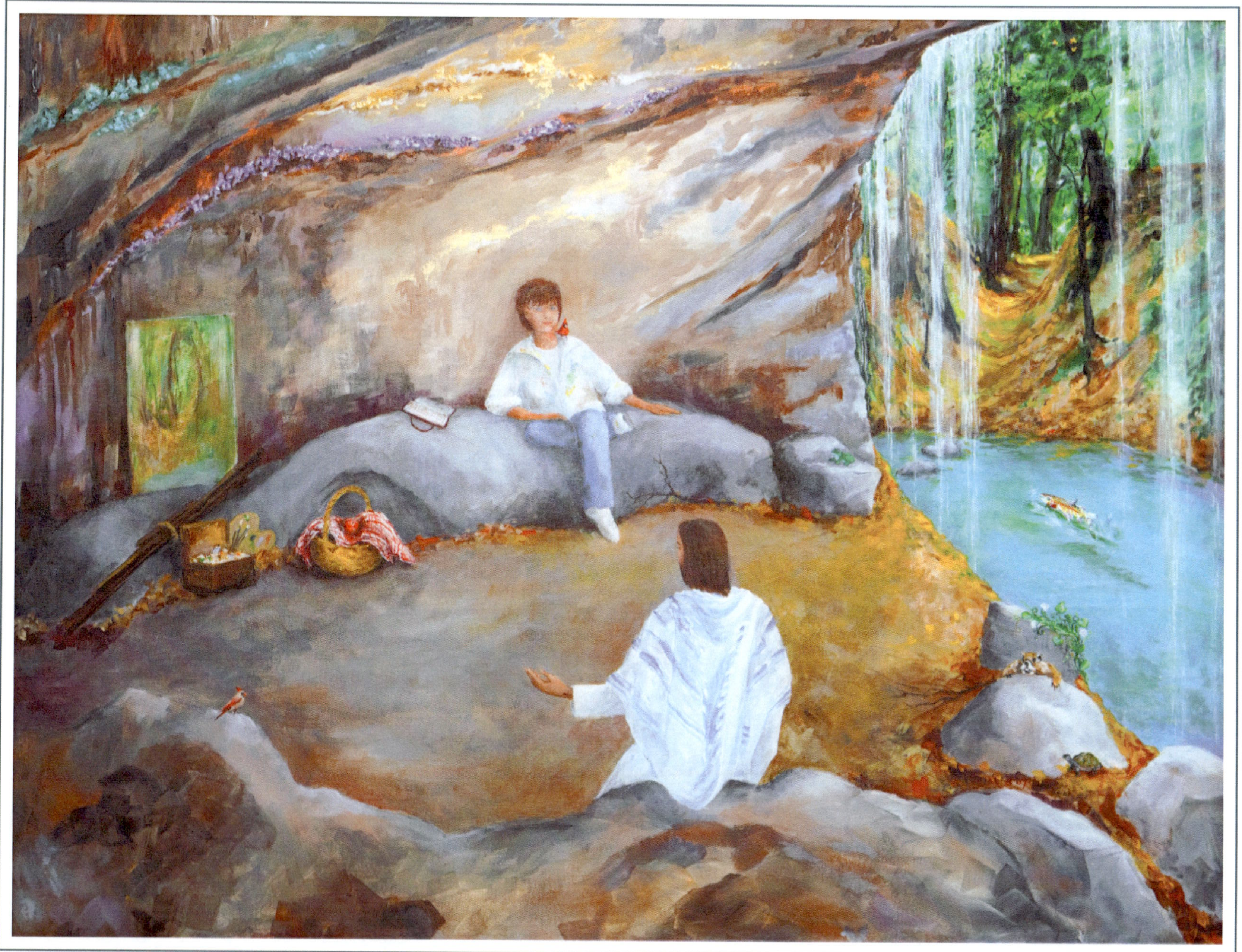

# The Inner Room

## The Painting

Hidden away, deep in a forest, where all is still except for the creatures that dwell there, is a cave carved into the side of a hill, partially obscured by a small waterfall. This cave is my prayer-room. It is a place made from favorite things: the cool touch of rock, the sound of water, and butterflies dancing in the sunlight. I carry this room with me at all times. "But you, when you pray, go into your inner room, and when you have shut your door, pray to your Father who is in secret, and your Father who sees in secret will repay you" (Matthew 6:6).

## The Story

I close my eyes to pray and I hear the gentle waterfall. A cool, wet breeze touches my face from the curtain of water falling over the entrance; I open my eyes to my inner room. I am leaning against a wall of rock, embedded with veins of gold, amethyst, and emerald, treasures revealed to me as I studied the precious words in my Bible. It is open beside me, waiting, there is so much more.

Often, I stand on my cave's sofa to reach up and touch these riches, recalling warm memories: the pure gold of leaning on Jesus when life seemed cold and too hard to endure—it was then that He took my hand in His. A vein of purple and violet amethyst, for the beauty He has shown me where before I saw only ugliness. Emerald, sparkling green for the pure joy of His acceptance—not the rejection I feared when first we met. I am safe within the solid rock of my inner room; Jesus is The Rock, and embedded in Him is every good and perfect thing.

I brought a picnic basket. It is covered with a red-checkered cloth, and a juicy, red apple waits on top. Next to the basket is a container of art supplies. I laugh to myself at the difference in size between the two—one of my favorite things to do is eat. As always, His provision is perfect!

I am wearing my painting clothes today. Against the wall is a canvas I have started; a view of the trees and a path I can see across the water. Jesus has come to meet with me. After we talk for a while, I will set up my easel to paint. Jesus likes to sit and watch. He sometimes picks up a brush and adds a touch or two; now and again, He works until the painting is completed. When He paints, I watch quietly, learning.

Today, Jesus is wearing a prayer shawl over comfortable robes, the same robes worn long ago when He walked the streets of Jerusalem. His mother made these robes. Oftentimes, He wears an old shirt and jeans, making it easier to climb up into the cave. Sometimes I see Him arrive with sadness on His face. When He is dressed in shepherd's clothing and carrying His staff, I know our time together will involve some correction. He guides His sheep (like me) with His staff to keep them on secure paths. Behind every correction, there is love.

Have you noticed the very red cardinal sitting on my shoulder, and his softly colored mate on the rock near Jesus? A shy marmot peers over the top of a rock, the frog and a turtle sit very still, listening to Jesus's voice. There is a splash of color as a trout jumps from the water.

In my inner-room, nothing is off limits. Whoops of Joy echo against the walls. Thankfulness felt so deeply that words are of no use. I bring to Him all my heartache and fear, knowing He will take them away and rest will come; many a time I have fallen asleep on the earth floor, quite content.

I look up at you, just for a second, to say goodbye.

I hope this painting encourages you to spend time designing your own inner prayer room. Awesome times are ahead; He created you with treasures and talents that are yours alone and eagerly waits to show them to you. One day I hope to hear about them, or see them in your own artwork. Until then, may our every thought be a prayer to our Father, in the name above all names, Jesus.

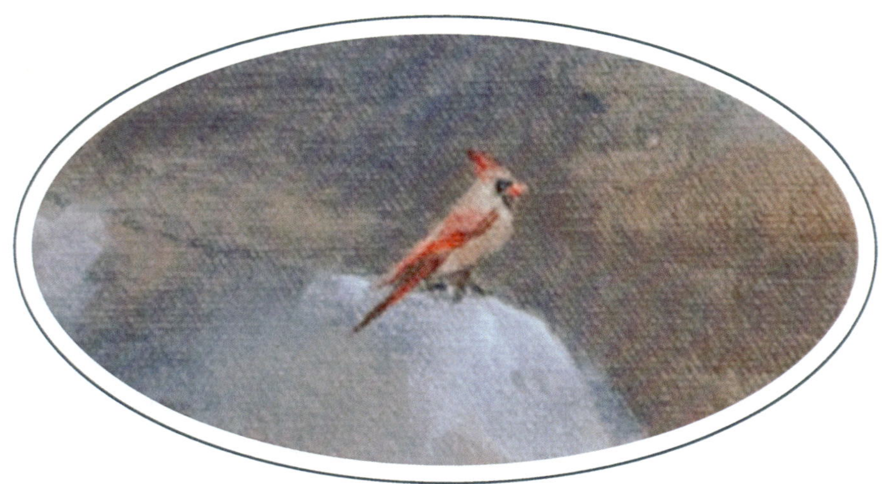

# His Hands

I sat staring at my blank computer screen and drifted off, daydreaming. "What if I were able to see through the eyes of a small brown mouse in the home of Joseph the Carpenter?" Instantly a carousel of living scenes revolves in my mind, and I hear calliope music!

Each scene, captured in few words. You and I are like two little brown mice, watching ….

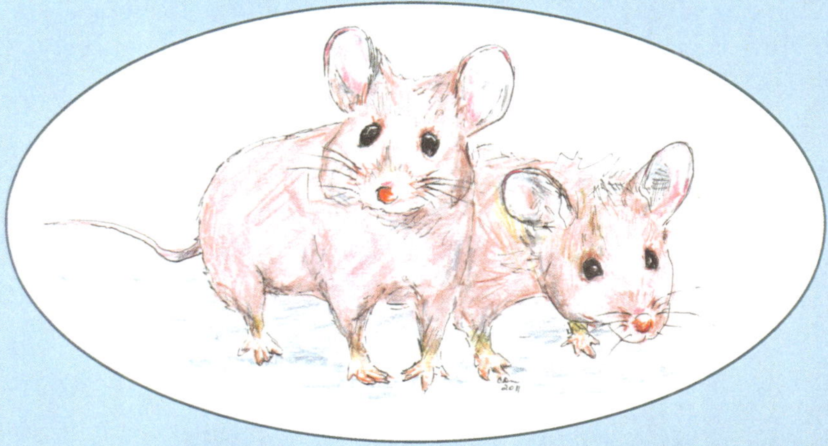

Little chubby baby hands reach up to touch His mother's face. Mary hugs her baby tightly, with tickles and giggles. His name is Jesus.

~ ~ ~ ~ ~

Young hands that play with hand-carved toys, made by a loving father. Laughter fills their home. Three hearts, filled with love.

(I smile as I type; the journey of His hands starts with much happiness.)

~ ~ ~ ~ ~

Youthful, determined hands that become rough and bruised while learning the carpenter's trade. Jesus's hands are marked with cuts, scrapes, and occasionally, the miss-aimed blow of a hammer. Days filled with the closeness of working with his earthly father.

~ ~ ~ ~ ~

Now a teenager running free over the hills, His arms outstretched, hands catching the wind. I wonder if Jesus knows that all of this is His creation. In this small village it is late afternoon. Jesus talks and laughs with friends, jostling and wrestling, until His mother calls that their evening meal is ready.

In the synagogue, His finger traces words written on holy scrolls, telling and foretelling of the dealings between God and man. I wonder, does He know?

~ ~ ~ ~ ~

Now grown, these hands gather chosen men, motioning to them … *Follow Me.*

~ ~ ~ ~ ~

A young girl lays dead. Jesus takes her hand, speaking words of life. He restores her to grieving parents, *all joy.*

~ ~ ~ ~ ~

In a grove of olive trees His hands lift in prayer, His heart is trembling … the will of the Father—His will.

~ ~ ~ ~ ~

These same hands do not flinch or move away, that day on a hill called Calvary. It is not the soldiers, and it is not the nails, that hold him. It is His steeled love for you and me. He knows our souls are on the balancing scale, and will not move from His Father's plan.

The Father places on His Son the sins of the world, then turns away … and breaks His own heart. There has never been, nor ever will be, a darkness so deep.

Jesus cries out, "My God, My God, why hast Thou forsaken Me?" (Matthew 27:46b).

~ ~ ~ ~ ~

Hands drop in death. The price of sin … PAID in FULL.

~ ~ ~ ~ ~

In the cold tomb, lay lifeless hands.

~ ~ ~ ~ ~

Then, wonder of wonders, He is alive! I look at His wounded hands, now extended toward me, and my first instinct is to care for and bandage them. I am completely taken aback when, instead of bloodied bandages, His hands contain a kingly gift wrapped in the finest white linen and reddest of ribbons. He motions for me to take the gift. I stand as if in a dream, my body frozen, my heart screaming, "Yes!" He bends down and places His gift into my hands—our hands—for there is one for each of us. Jesus watches, a "hurry up" smile on His face, as first the ribbon is untied, and then my nervous fingers carefully unfold the linen. When I lift the lid and look inside, I see eternity through the eyes of my Savior—eternity with Him.

~ ~ ~ ~ ~

All of a sudden, *thump.* I am back sitting at my computer. I have started to type, "THE END." But wait. I am now the one smiling. "Thou wilt make known to me the path of life; in Thy presence is fullness of joy; in Thy right hand there are pleasures forever" (Psalm 16:11). Jesus's gift *has no end.*

I am surprised to see you with your gift still unopened. I cannot imagine why you hesitate.

Jesus is waiting.

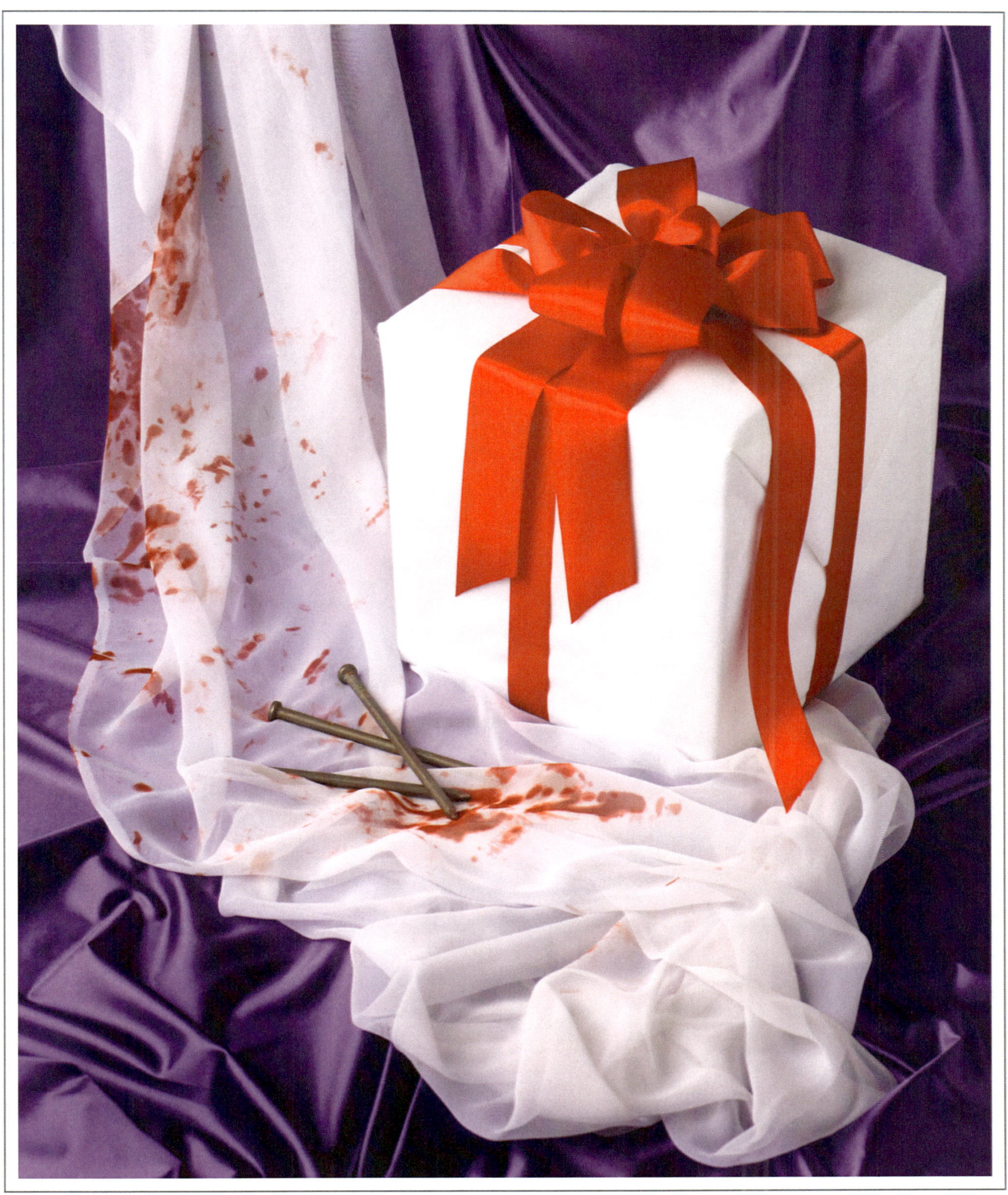

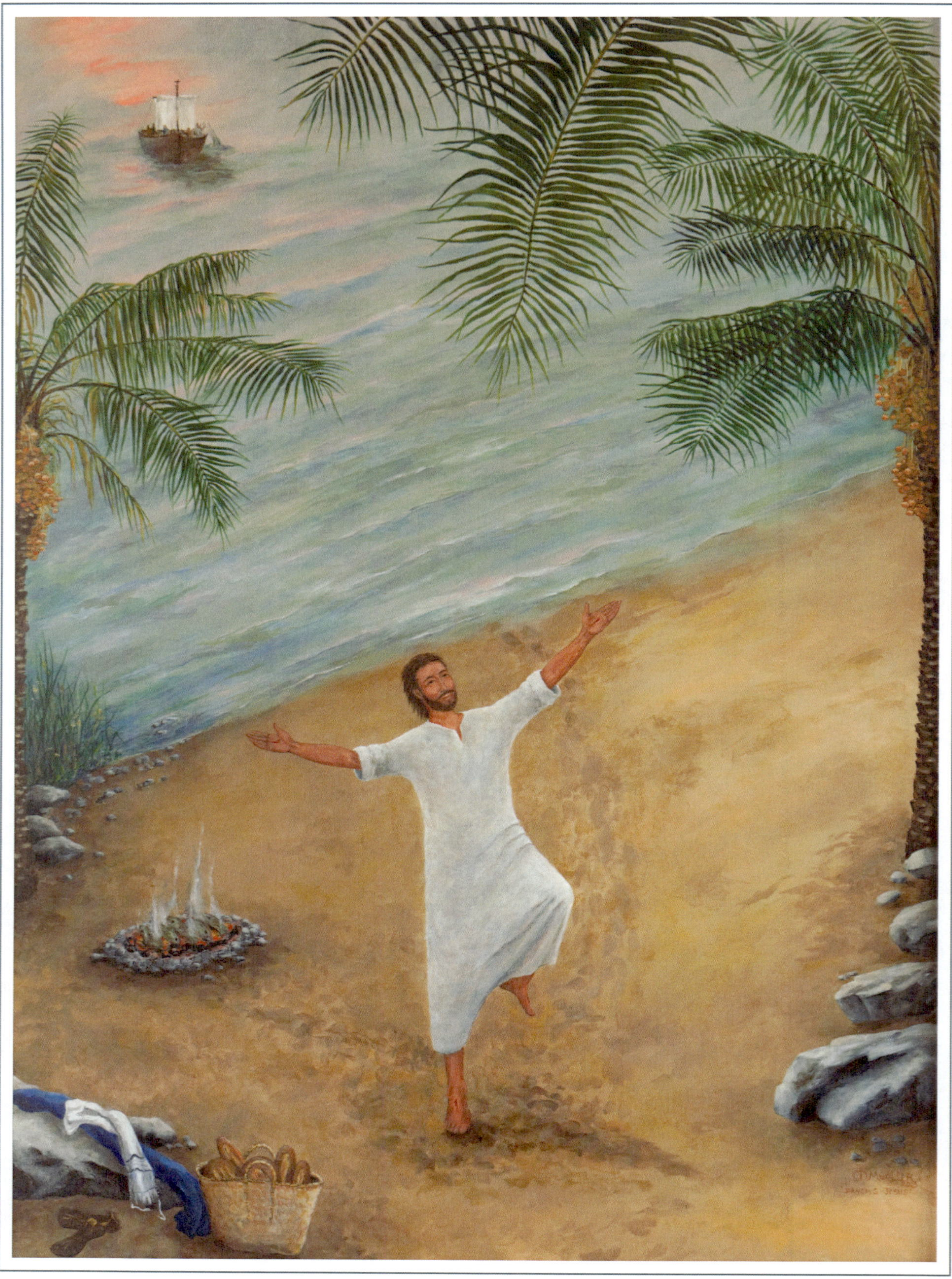

# Jesus Dancing

## The Painting

Only the lapping of the waves, washing against the shore, disturbs the quiet morning. Jesus stands, looking out across the Sea of Galilee, and feeling the breeze cool on his face. The sun rises from the water, color spreading across the sky, reminding Him of home. He misses His Father. The work He was sent to do is ending.

He places His outer garments on a large rock and takes off His sandals. The sand crunches between His toes. He raises His arms, throws back his head to shout and begins to dance to the rhythm of the music in His heart—there on the beach, a young man, joy-filled. Then He catches a glimpse of the wounds in his hands and remembers … the taunting, yelling, angry faces. He also remembers John holding His mother, and the ache in their eyes.

The smell of the fish on the coals brings Him back to the present. He looks out at the sea again, watching the old fishing boat rocking on the water as His disciples throw out their fishing nets. He senses the churning of their souls, the confusion of loss and defeat, the weight of shame and guilt. Their nets are thrown in the air with none of the old vigor of working side-by-side, and no laughter fills the air. The waves bring the fishing boat closer and closer to shore; soon, a voice they thought forever gone will call out to them.

Jesus looks up as the palm trees rustle in the quickening breeze, announcing His Father's presence. His human heart pounds with emotion. The Father has come down to look upon His Beloved Son after His suffering, to intently look upon Him, and make sure He is well. Jesus digs His toes into the sand and swings around, laughing out loud. Father, it is time! The waiting is over. Soon, my chosen ones will be able to hear me when I call out to them. They will come: Nathanael, John, Peter, and Thomas, all of them. The fish and bread are prepared and we will sit and eat together; the astonished look on their faces will turn to smiles and their heaviness will wash away.

Father, after breakfast I will be having that conversation with Simon Peter. Peter's mind is never far from that courtyard; he sees the fire where he warmed his hands, he hears his voice denying Me. He remembers My face turning to look at him; he is in deep anguish. Father, open his whole being to the healing words I will speak to him. Quiet him; so that the forgiveness he receives will sink deep into his soul, restoring the closeness of our friendship.

~ ~ ~ ~ ~

The meaning of this painting is, in many ways, obvious. Perhaps there are others for whom only the eyes of the heart will understand. May you come to that place, and dance on the beach with Jesus.

## *The Story*

This painting began when Laura, an artist friend of mine, quite decidedly told me, "Your next painting should be of Jesus, dancing." I dismissed this with, "No! Unheard of! 'Tradition!'" (I sounded like an echo from *Fiddler on the Roof*). My thinking was that certainly Jesus should be painted doing something holy—not *dancing*.

During the next couple of months, pictures flooded my mind of an old fishing boat and the sun just coming up over the water; of Jesus, barefoot on the sand. Soon these thoughts invaded my heart to the point where I knew. Yes. I was to paint Jesus dancing, and to paint Him doing something holy. What could possibly be more holy than a Father and Son loving each other?

This painting took over a year to finish. There were countless times when I wondered, "Does the Father *really* want this painting of His Son?" When I thought about presenting Jesus in this unconventional way, I must admit that I had become afraid—afraid of being rejected of men. The Holy Spirit, in His infinite patience, repeatedly brought encouragement into my life.

I was sitting in church one Sunday having a gray day; this is a day when nothing seems right and everything is a bit muddled. Suddenly my mind cleared; the choir was singing, "I came down from heaven and I danced on the earth."[1] It was all I could do to contain myself. They sang of Jesus coming down from heaven and dancing on earth. My heart exploded in the realization that the Father had had them sing for me, the one who had lost her courage. They sang for me to keep on keeping on. All joy broke loose inside of me.

---

1 From "Lord of the Dance" Words and Music by Sydney Carter. Copyright 1963 Stainer & Bell Ltd. London, England. Tune is an adaptation of Shaker melody "Simple Gifts" same copyright holder.

I had been telling my sister Bonnie about my painting, so when she came for a visit it was a brief "Hello", a hug, and then a quick walk to the room where I paint. I heard a loud gasp and I ran, thinking something had happened to her. Standing in front of the canvas, she said, "I've always pictured Jesus hanging on a cross, battered and bloody. Now, to see Him free and happy has freed me." I was humbled, and very thankful.

A few months later, and about six months into the painting, I was going through some pamphlets I had picked up at an arts' seminar. Inside one was a poem titled, "The Resurrection Breakfast, Jesus: John 21," by Tanya Runyan. I read her words, "I hear my loved ones talking in a rickety boat, behind the pink mist of daybreak …."

"It's my painting!" I gasped. The scriptures I had been reading as painting research were now in front of me as poetry; the two were *one*. I called the number on the pamphlet and asked for Tanya's telephone number. I was told, "I'm so sorry, we don't have it." I left my number, just in case, and said a prayer. The next morning, a very excited receptionist called me back: "You won't believe this, but Tanya called here this morning; she said to give you her number."

I sent a big "thank you" up to heaven. Our Father tucks these small blessings into our lives, to cheer us on and to give us hope. Was my call to Tanya important? Yes. Her pen had been sitting idle for a long time. As for me, I picked up my paintbrush.

~ ~ ~ ~ ~

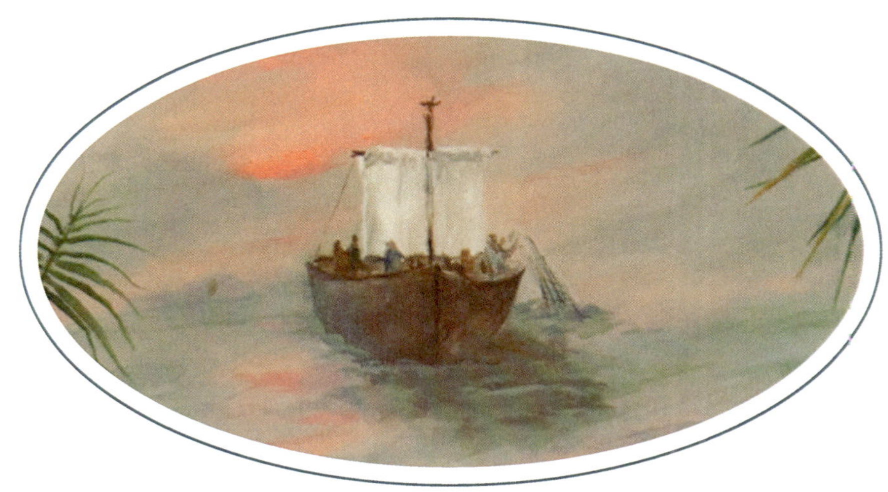

# The Resurrection Breakfast, Jesus: John 21

Even starting a simple fire
is amazing to me now,
this flint a vague dream
I know everything about.
I let the flames blow along my skin
like soft desert poppies,
watch the coals glow
through the open puckers of flesh
in my hands.

I hear my loved ones
talking in a rickety boat
behind the pink mist of daybreak,
and I know who that is suddenly leaps
to the water when I speak,
tunic spreading around him
like a thinning cloud.
As Peter swims toward me,
my heart turns like a planet in my chest,
arms fall open to embrace this dream
from another life, from yesterday.
I love his sunburned face,
always wrinkled from
so much thought and surprise,
hair slick on the neck, eyes determined
to keep me from vanishing.

As he nears shore, he sees smoke –
bread and fire at my feet!
He charges back to the boat
with all life, slinging the latest catch
over his shoulder.

Trudging back smiling,
he grows from the waves;
his muscles strain
with dozens of squirming fish,
their gills sputtering water in the air.

At the sand's edge he reaches
his hands out for balance.
He holds on so tight, I can feel
the blood pressing through each
capillary, the thickness of
each nerve twitching
in his fingertips.
My old body never felt this much –
the oxygen whispering in the cells,
the nuclei spinning in orbit.
The beautiful edges of his soul
loosening and falling,
small golden scales
sticking in my scars.

Tanya Runyan
*(used with permission)*

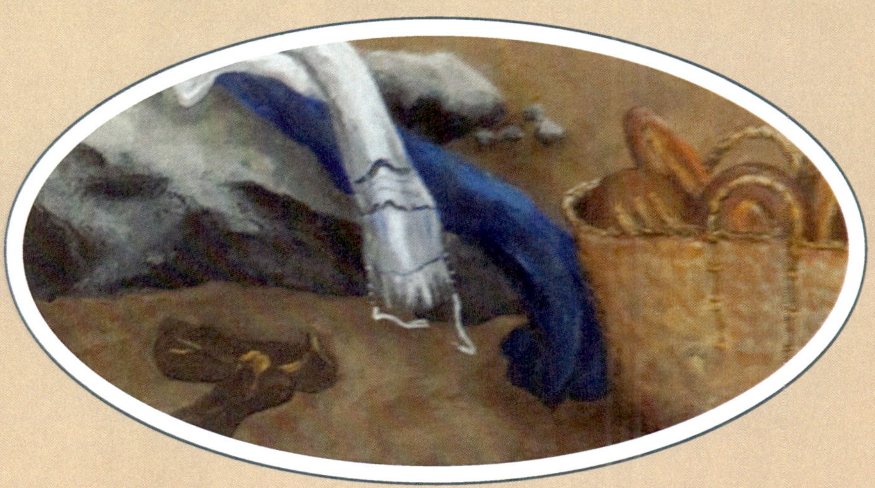

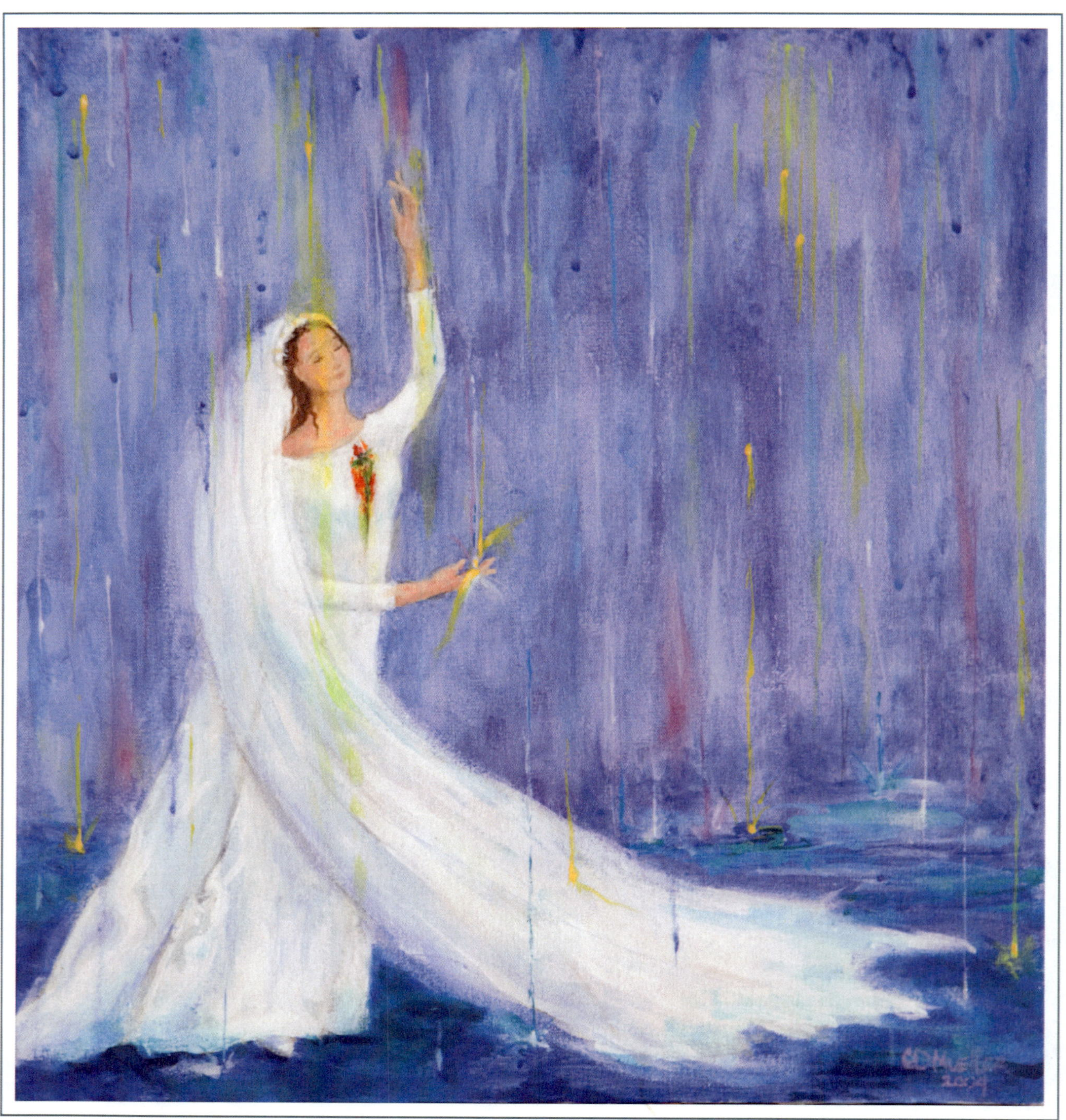

# Worshipping Warrior

## The Painting

Her satin dress is heavy with the downpour. Her veil, soaked, trails on the ground. The rain is coming down from the Father of lights. "Every good thing bestowed and every perfect gift is from above, coming down from the Father of lights, with whom there is no variation, or shifting shadow" (James 1:17). The raindrops are every imaginable color, for every imaginable need. Her long fingers are extended to catch this gift from heaven. She stands as if in a river of life.

## The Story

This painting was created at the request of a young guitarist named Sue Emmett. I hoped it would become the cover for the C.D. she was working on titled, "Worshipping Warrior." I was to illustrate "the Bride of Christ." As I painted, God's response to Sue was both a painting and a message. When I delivered the painting, the following letter accompanied it:

*"Dearest Sue,*

*As you can see, there have been many changes from our original discussion about how the bride should be depicted. I followed strong promptings as I painted; to add this, and to change that. When the painting was near completion I started to study it, and without warning, I broke down sobbing uncontrollable tears. Love was being poured out toward you from Jesus and His Father. Overwhelming love, I felt as though my heart would burst. Finally, quietness came and I was able to compose myself. Tears had fallen on the brush I was using and had mixed with the paint; I used this brush to finish the canvas.*

*I knew that, through this painting, God was giving you something amazing, a tangible gift to look at and to hold. A touch point when all seems lost and you find no love in your heart … for yourself. You are to remember that you are His chosen vessel, an instrument to bless others. Just as you hold your guitar, the Father holds you. Lifting people through worship and prophetic words, you place them gently on the doorstep of heaven. So many times, I have closed my eyes, listened to your song, and peace has come into my troubled world. My heart is full with the words that came to me; they are as much a part of this painting as the paint itself."*

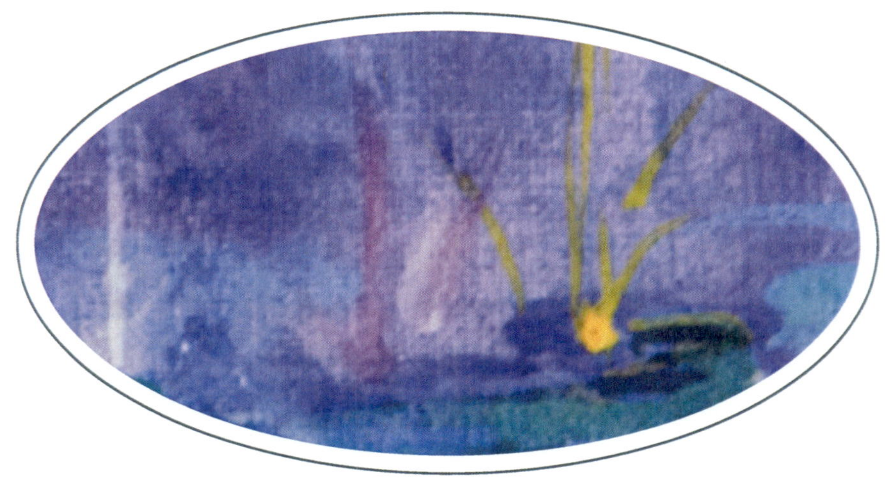

"Sue,
As you begin to worship Me
and lead the ones gathered round,
My heart is touched with your desire,
their expectancy and great need.
See the sky open
raining My mercy and healing,
filling them,
filling them,
filling them.
The rain becomes a river of life
as you speak My words to them,
as you sing My truth.
They are My bride,
and you are my joy, my little one.
The fire you spoke of to Charlene
has become a beautiful red rose.
It has been placed in and over your heart,
ever ready to bloom at My bidding.
You will ever be, My worshiping warrior.
I Am, and will ever be,
your Abba, Father."

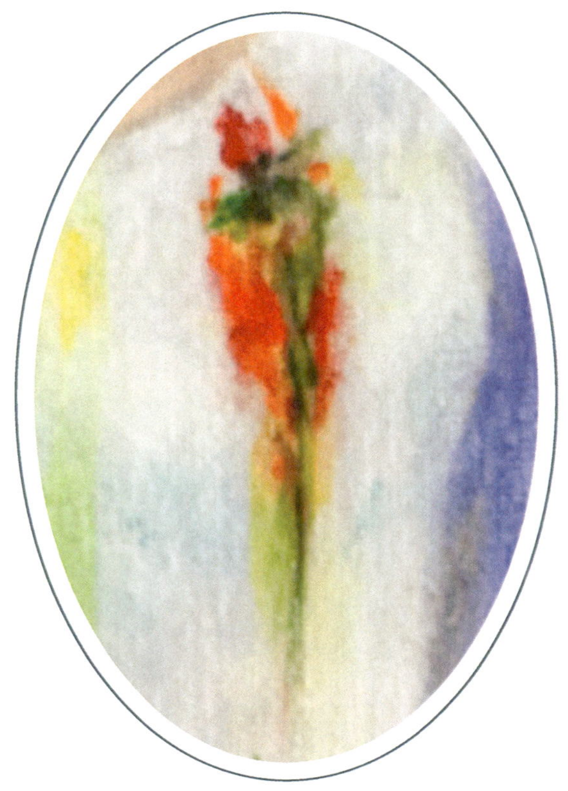

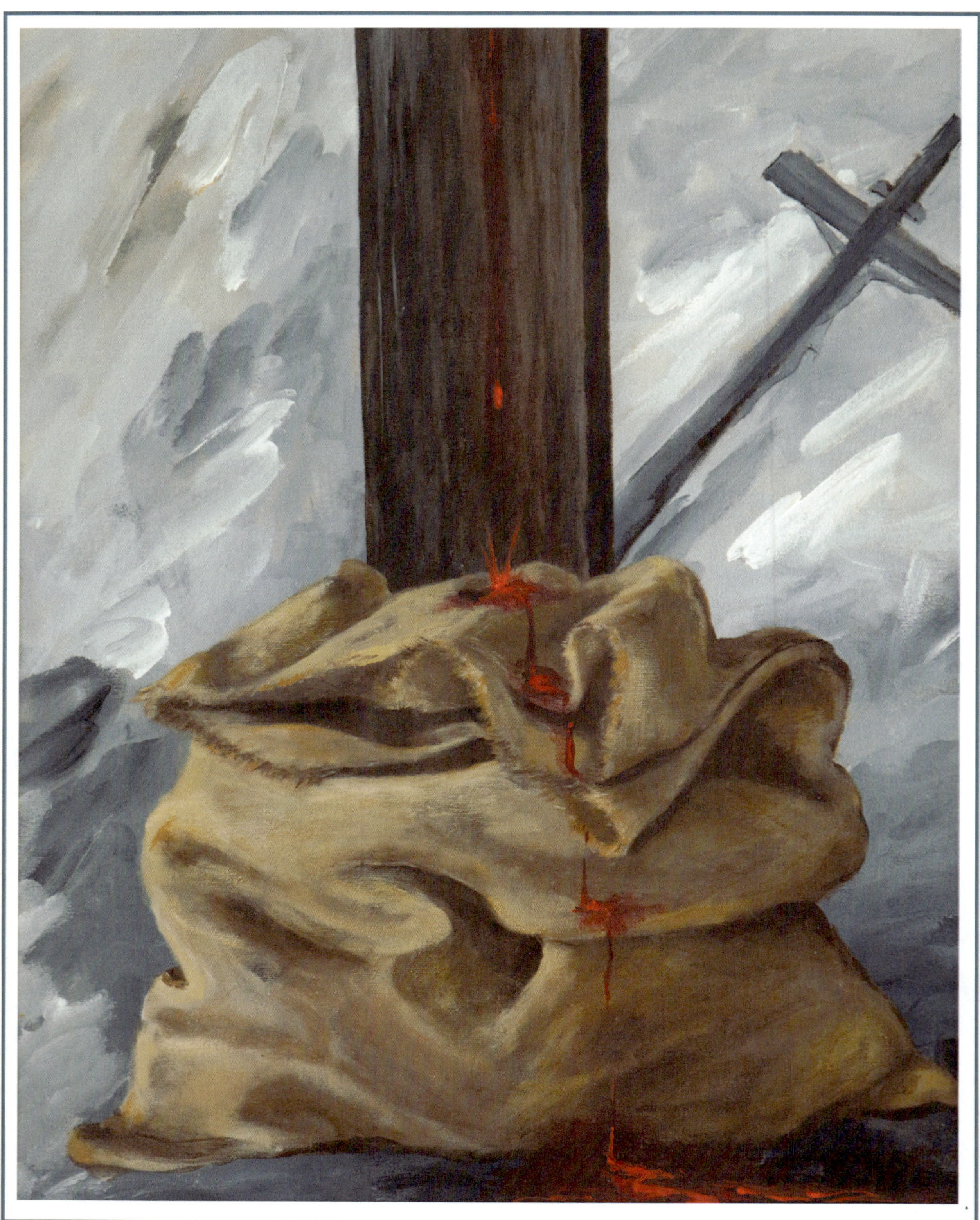

# He Covers Me

## The Painting

An old burlap bag leans against the cross. With a frown, you think, "What is that old, grubby sack doing there?" You see the blood that has soaked into the wood, the blood falling onto the bristly cloth and running down each fold, then onto the earth. Your eyes want to stay fixed near the ground. To raise them and see Jesus's broken body struggling to breathe, would demand your full strength. Weakness has overtaken you.

A shadow of the cross is cast against a sky so agitated; it seems as if there are angels wrestling scornful demons in defense of Jesus.

You hear, "Father, forgive them; for they do not know what they are doing" (Luke 23:34a). Startled, you look up … .

## The Story

The first time I heard Jacqueline Meyer tell her story of how God freed her, I felt the old familiar "Holy Spirit nudge" that meant I was to put this vision on canvas, His gift to her.

Here are her words…

> "I was walking outside, during a time when I was spiritually and emotionally burdened about issues in my life. As I walked, the vision came forth (all in grays, without any color). I saw myself walking uphill carrying a large, heavy, burlap bag (my burdens). It was so heavy that it caused me to walk bent over. I struggled uphill, until I found myself standing at the base of the cross. I let loose of the bag; I let it fall against the cross and as I stepped back, bright red drops of blood began to splash upon my bag of burdens.

You have heard the phrase: "It's in the bag," when something is a sure thing, all taken care of. That phrase has taken on a completely new meaning for me. All my cares and worries are in the bag, under the blood—already taken care of!"

As you can see, this painting was not done in gray hues as Jacqueline beheld in her vision. When I asked permission to add color, she agreed and came to observe as I painted. The painting now hangs in the entryway of her home, framed in old barn-wood; a perfect fit.

When I feel weighed down by sin or circumstances, my imagination takes me into the place of the painting. At the foot of the cross, I kneel, moving the burlap sack aside. Sitting on the ground, leaning against the rough wood, He is near. Soon my troubled world hushes. He covers me.

~ ~ ~ ~ ~

You say *you* want to lean for a while. Here, let me move over. There is always room at the cross.

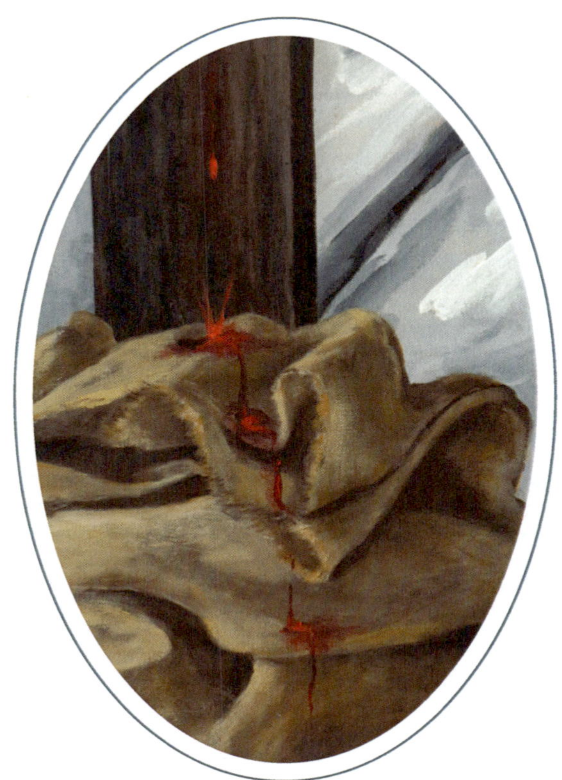

# Morning Prayer

O Great Redeemer,

is anything too difficult for You?

No.

The deepest pit,

the blackest hole,

for You—No Fear.

I must hold close to You.

Your holy eyes,

Your holy mind,

Your holy person,

snatching me from the Fire.

Your blood covering,

as a Father blanketing His child.

You did the difficult,

You did the Impossible,

You are truly,

GOD.

Help me surrender,

help me to see,

in this confusion called living.

I see the Glory,

on the edge of the terrible storm cloud.

Help me to be,

help me to set my cause

to follow only You.

You are,

GOD.

Just over the horizon,

I can see You.

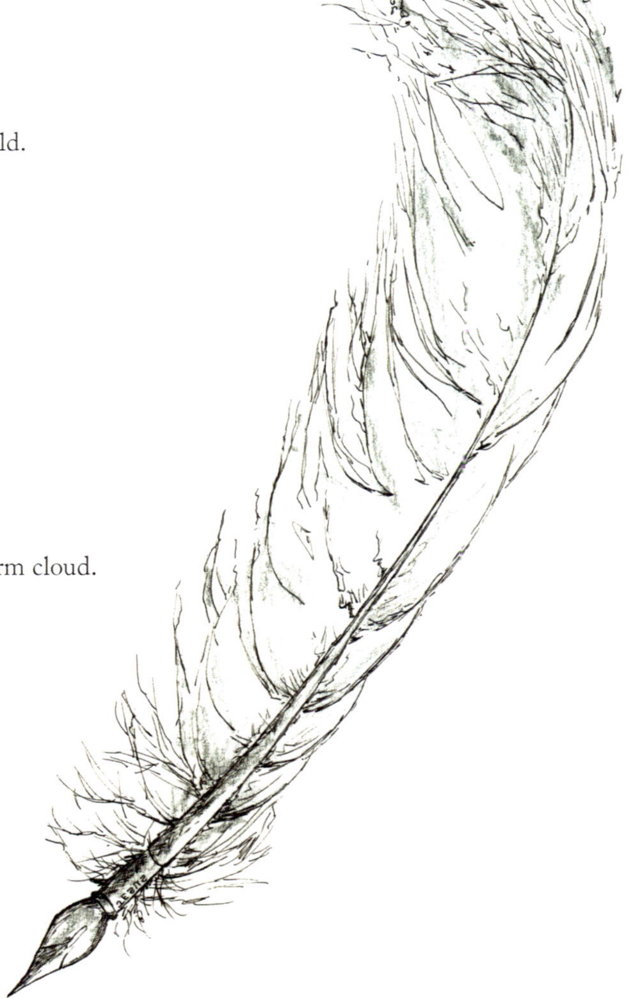

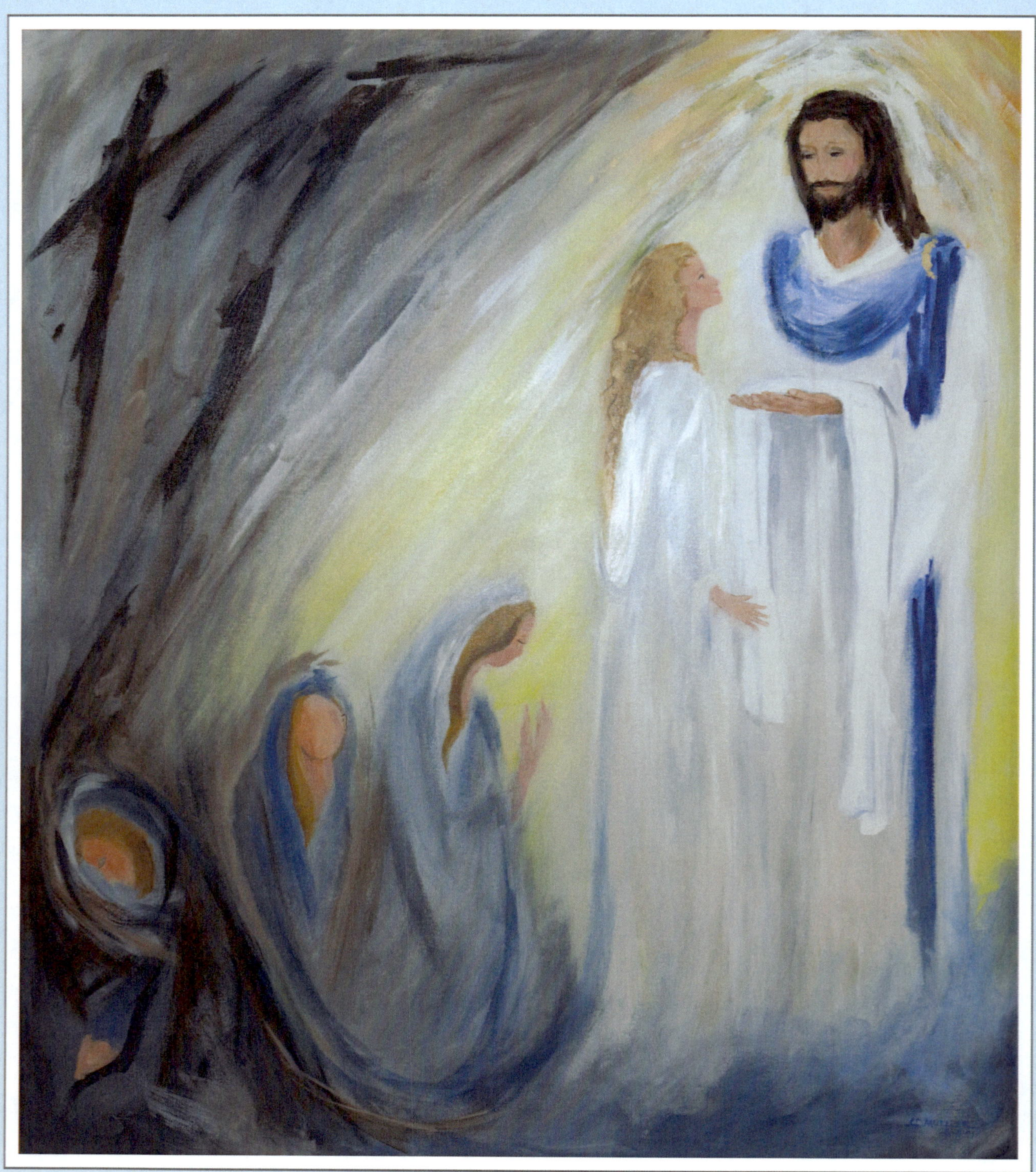

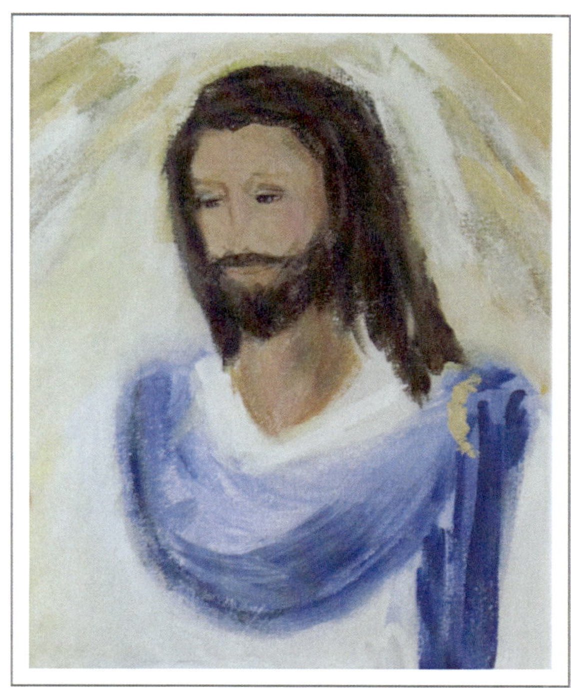

# The Quest

## The Painting

Roughly executed, this painting is nearer a sketch. It has an unfinished quality, compared to my usual style, and for a reason. On my first day of painting, when I stepped back to examine its progress, the expression in the eyes of Jesus caught my attention. I did not want to lose that lovingly intent gaze, and I knew that if I continued to paint, this might happen. I reviewed the work and established that all of the story-elements were in place. I added a few more strokes, and the large, gold, kingly brooch that Jesus is wearing. Then I put down my brush.

This painting tells of four phases in the life of a young woman, including the quest to rescue her.

Jesus looks into her eyes as she stands before Him. He sees the beginning, when first He called to her—and her answer was to run. As she ran, the glitter and the lies of this world swallowed her, piece by piece. The results of her choice left her feeling discarded, like a piece of worn-out clothing. The enemy battled for her, but at every twist and turn, he met the Cross. In the midnight of her flight, the light of Jesus continued to shine, cracking the ice that encased her heart. Now on her knees, the willful pride that had brought her low is revealed. The ice melts.

When Jesus calls for the second time, she turns to listen. There are no facial features painted, only an ear. This time Jesus's words find a welcome home; now she understands, and believes.

With head bowed and still on her knees, she fully turns to Jesus. Tears fall. These tears are both sadness for the pain her sin has caused and wonder at the new life that now fills her.

She stands before Jesus and timidly lifts the eyes of her heart to meet His. In an instant, all traces of fear drain from her being. Gone are the memories of rejection buried deep within her. Shame is no more—it is covered with mercy. Grace melts away unmerciful self-reproach. As forgiveness reigns, the past is no more.

She sees Jesus lift a snow-white garment and, without hesitation, (before a question can enter her mind), the King wraps His robe of righteousness about her shoulders. It completely envelops her; she is a new creation.

"I will rejoice greatly in the Lord,

My soul will exult in my God;

For He has clothed me with garments of salvation,

He has wrapped me with a robe of righteousness"

(Isaiah 61:10a).

Later when her astonishment subsides, she rests on her bed and tries to imagine the future. A small frown of old worry appears on her brow, but this quickly disappears as the soft sound of music drifts into her consciousness; she falls into a deep sleep.

"The Lord will command His lovingkindness in the daytime;

And His song will be with me in the night,

A prayer to the God of my life"

(Psalm 42:8).

~ ~ ~ ~ ~

Jesus's quest to capture her heart ends in victory. May this be so for everyone who hears His voice.

# Isaiah 1:18

## The Painting

With a large brush to lay down bold strokes, I painted. This piece represents the working out of the gift of Repentance—the recognition, the understanding, the laying of ourselves down in the dust, in heartfelt agreement with the enormity of our sin.

See the blood of Jesus tearing up and through—then flowing over the live coals of sin until they collapse. The colors are thick, deep, and heavy; I want you to feel the heat, smell the acrid fumes, to grasp in some small measure, the cost of sin.

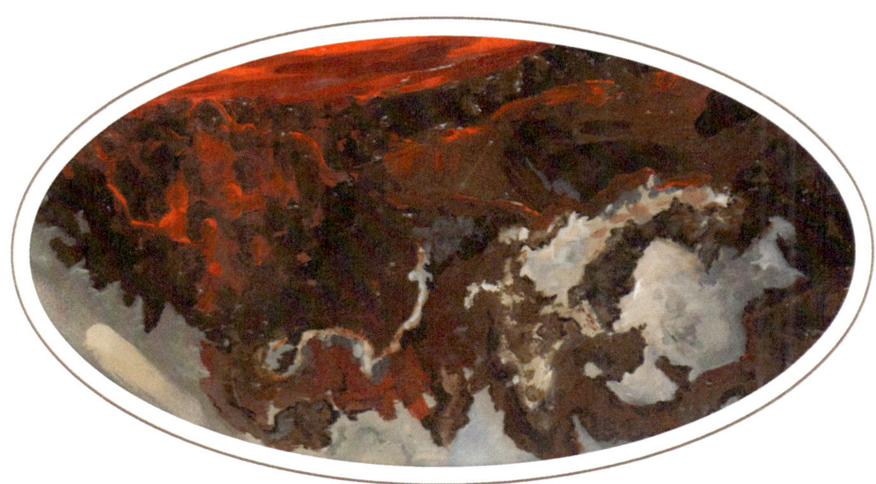

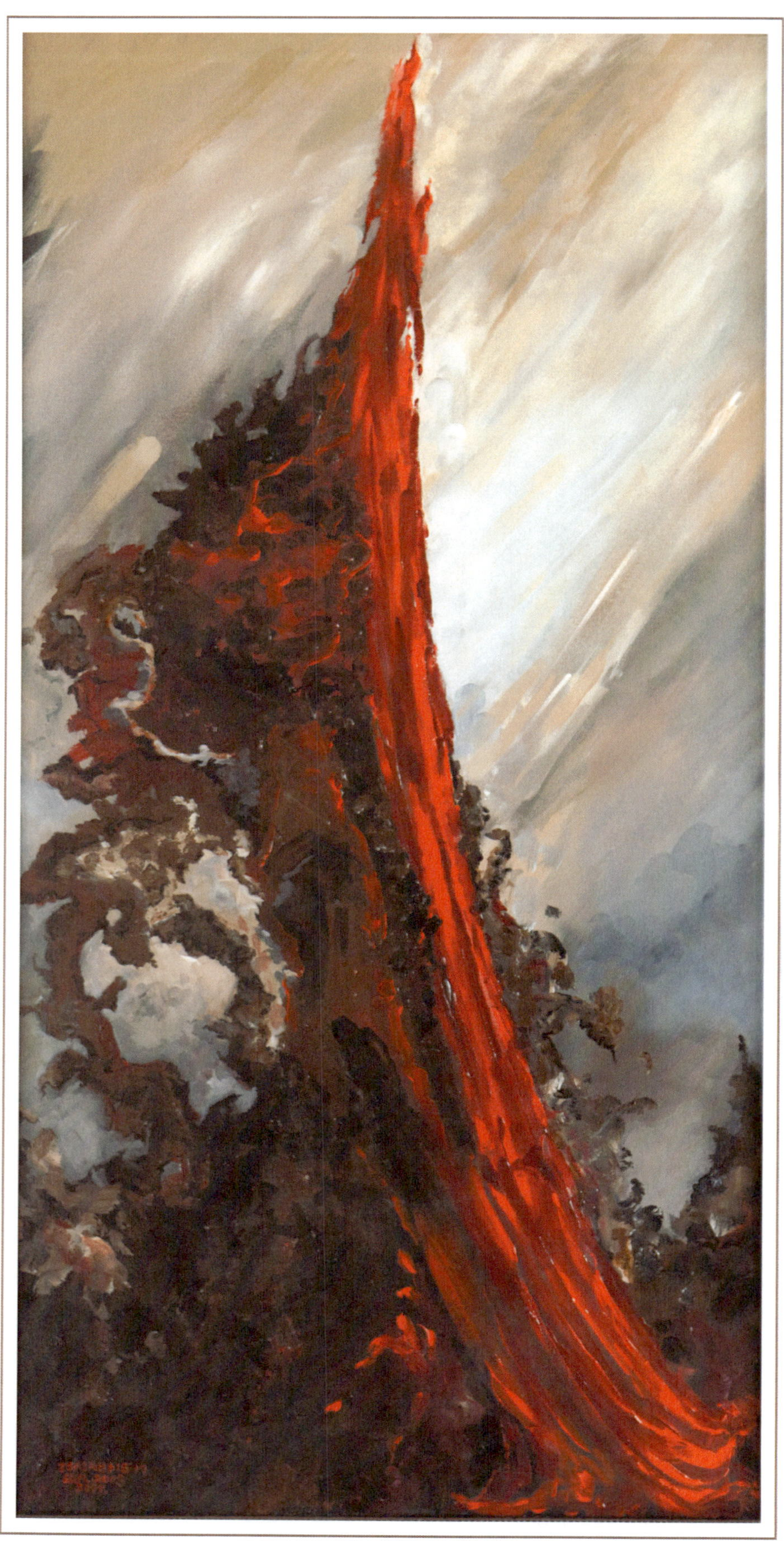

A long, long, time ago, in a faraway garden, a great yawning chasm opened between God and man. "And the Lord God commanded the man, saying, 'From any tree of the garden you may eat freely; but from the tree of the knowledge of good and evil you shall not eat, for in the day that you eat from it you shall surely die'" (Genesis 2:16-17). Adam and Eve yielded to temptation and ate from the forbidden tree. Spiritual death came to them and, through them, to every child born to man.

For the very first time, Adam and Eve experienced guilt and fear. "And they heard the sound of the Lord God walking in the garden in the cool of the day, and the man and his wife hid themselves from the presence of the Lord God among the trees of the garden" (Genesis 3:8). When the Lord God questioned Adam and Eve, instead of admitting what they had done, blame issued from their mouths. Finally, the judgments fell: upon the serpent (that Satan used to bring the temptation), upon Eve and Adam, and upon the earth itself.

They stand *outside*; barred from entering the garden they love. The closeness with their God, their friend … broken. The chambers of their hearts echo the emptiness. Sin, as a dull knife has slashed God's wonderful canvas, the colors smeared, the design ruined.

~ ~ ~ ~ ~

In the foreknowledge of God, and before (the creation of the garden), God knew man would fall into sin. A plan, a way across the great chasm is put forth, a plan with a "staggering task" described in full detail. Jesus takes up the assignment. Salvation comes to us with a heavy price: His shed blood. Jesus is our living bridge to the Father, "Behold, the Lamb of God who takes away the sin of the world!" (John 1:29b).

~ ~ ~ ~ ~

I turn in my Bible to where it is written:

"Come now, and let us reason together,"

Says the Lord,

"Though your sins are as scarlet,

They will be as white as snow;

Though they are red like crimson,

They will be like wool"

(Isaiah 1:18).

I look again at the painting. It has not changed, *but my heart sees a different scene:* the sky is now clear of the burning and the smoke. My sins are no more; a blanket of white covers the ground. The canvas of my life is again clean and ready. Thankfulness fills me.

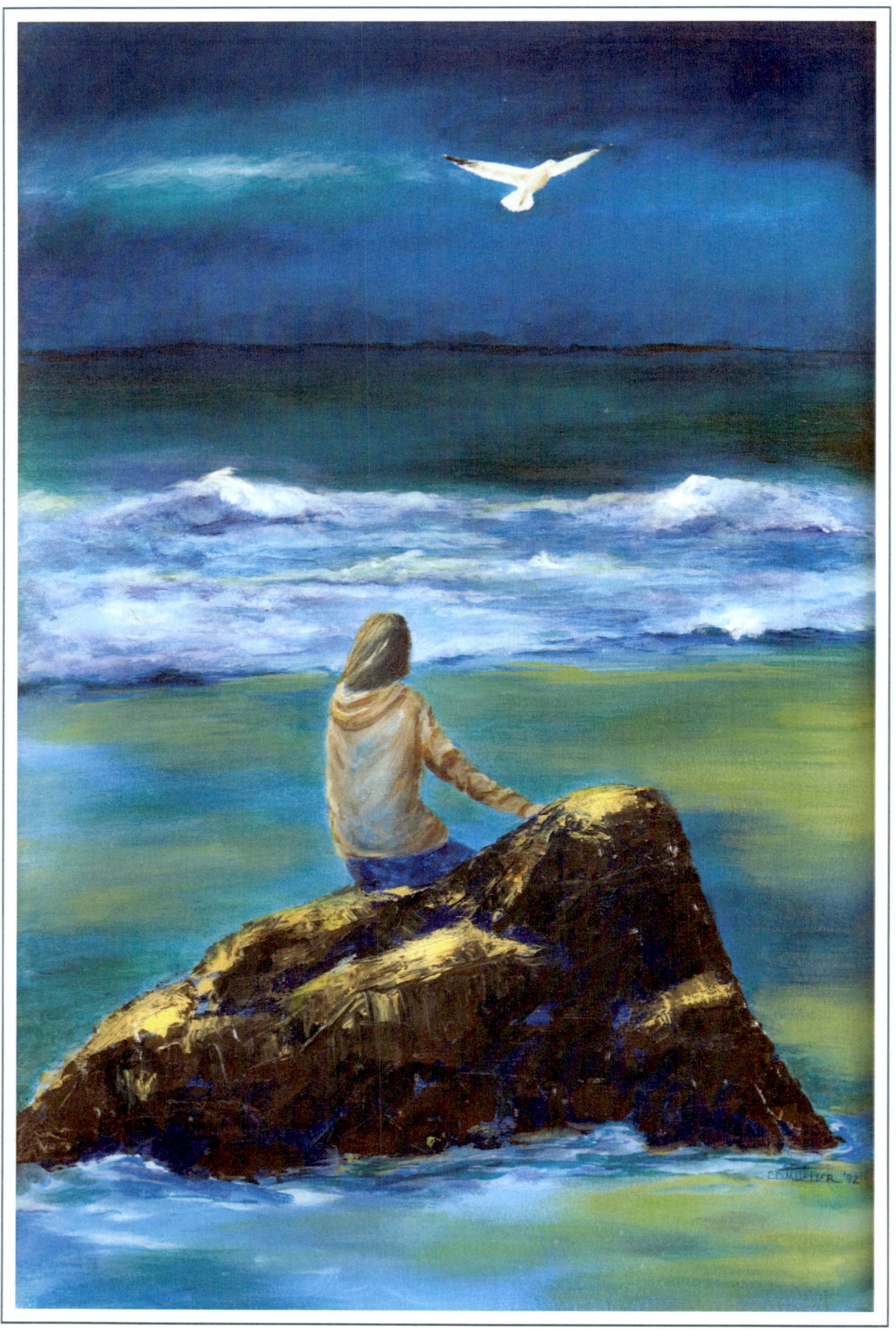

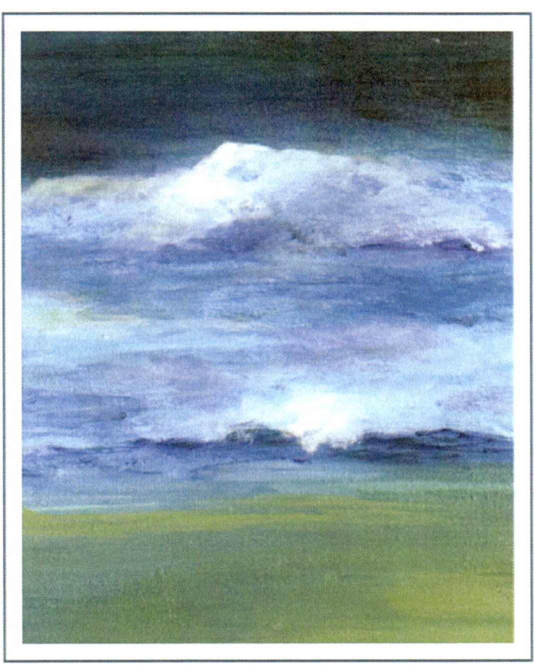

# Surprised by God

## The Paintings' Story – Part I

A girl wades out to a lonely rock near the shore and rests against it. The water swirling around her bare feet keeps her senses alive. She tries to lose herself in her surroundings, the deep, blue color of dusk, the piercing call of the sea gull, the salt spray of the ocean waves, but there is no escape. How could this have happened! She shudders, feeling cold—not physically cold—but soul-cold. The "blame game" starts in her mind. "It is entirely their fault—if she hadn't—if he would have …," but she knows the accusations are false. She alone has caused the deep hurt and separation in her family.

"I feel as if nothing matters." Hope has fled; her heart is like a fragile, empty glass. She feels its fall, then the shattering into a thousand pieces, like Humpty Dumpty, never to be put back together again.

But God ....

# A Personal Story

Let me tell you a story from my own life.

First, I have a question: Have you ever been faced with temptation, and fallen? I have. The guilt and distress squeezed my insides with an awful question, *How can God forgive me?* I had sinned against someone; I had sinned against my God. I wondered: *If I call, will He hear me; are the heavens now shut to me?* Fear was having a heyday, entangling my mind in cords of disbelief; disbelief in the forgiveness I knew to be true.

Suddenly, a little girl stood before me, her pretty flowered dress dripping with filth. My heart knew; I was the little girl, and the filth was sin. I stared at her for the longest time. Finally, I saw a large hand—God's hand—come near and pick me up by the back of my dress. He dunked me, up and down, up and down, in a large bowl of warm, soapy water. I was then well rinsed in another bowl of clean water, lifted up, and held there, dripping. A giant-sized blow dryer finished the job of my spiritual cleanup. As I watched, I could not help but smile.

In my despair, God had given me kindness; knowing my need, He had acted on my behalf. I have never forgotten the seriousness of my position as a sinner. I understand how incredibly kind He is, and how compassionate. I will be forever grateful.

I am old enough to remember my mother using a bar of Fels Naphtha soap; rubbing hard on a stain, and then using her washboard to torture that stain into surrender. In a spiritual sense, the innocent blood of Jesus is the soap; the cross is the washboard—the torture used to remove sin.

This story is bookmarked on my heart. You might use it yourself; to offer to someone you know who needs its comfort. Jesus loves to look down and watch as we share His love with others. I can see His chest puffed out, His fingers plucked under His suspenders, as He walks around heaven, saying, "That's my kid down there!"

Forgiveness is the wellspring of all good on this earth; it must intertwine all those whose lives belong to Him.

I will end my story with a favorite scripture: "The Lord God is my Strength, my personal bravery, and my invincible army; He makes my feet like hinds' feet and will make me to walk [not to stand still in terror, but to walk] and make [spiritual] progress upon my high places [of trouble, suffering, or responsibility]!" (Habakkuk 3:19 The Amplified Bible).

He is above, and beyond ... all desiring, all thirst.

# The Paintings' Story – Part II

The girl lifts her hands in shame to cover her face, then stops short. She sees, running over her palms like film from a silent movie, the sins of her life—sins of the past and this new sin, which causes the pain inside her to deepen. She stares, unable to look away.

A voice, quiet at first, becomes louder with each repeating: "Throw your sins into My ocean!" It is as if her arms are seized by an invisible force, preventing her from moving. She knows the voice of Jesus and fights to obey. With a great surge of strength—not hers alone—all her sins are hurled into the sea.

Her body slides down the rock and into the water. She struggles to her feet and scans the ocean looking for her sins, all she sees are the waves rolling in. She is tired, bruised, and wet—but she is laughing, for her heart is as a crystal chalice filled with hope and Jesus's love.

She sobers, thinking of her family. *Today I will go to them, asking humbly for their pardon.* The story comes full circle; all relationships, restored.

"Behold, the Lord's hand

is not so short

That it cannot save;

Neither is His ear so dull

That it cannot hear"

(Isaiah 59:1).

*Hope and Forgiveness.*

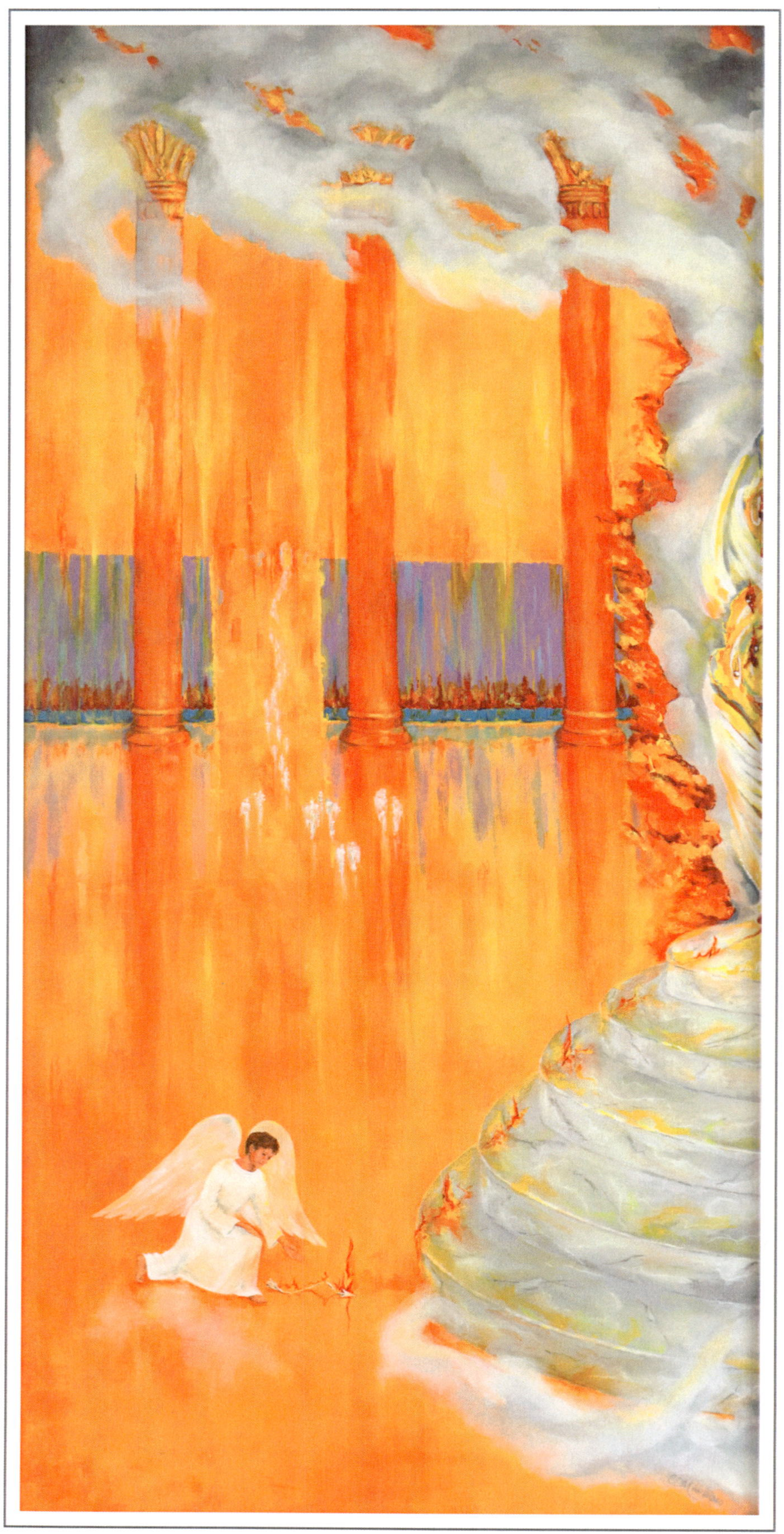

# Assignment: Silver Arrow

## The Painting

A somewhat crumpled and tarnished silver arrow takes flight from earth. Clattering on the floor of heaven, it slides across seamless perfection and comes to a stop at the foot of the Father's throne.

The small arrow catches the Father's attention. Every morning, He waits for it. The arrow is a prayer for help from one of His children; the answer is ready. Licks of holy fire flash down the stairs and onto the arrow—"Go, bring the help, bring the mercy to My waiting child." The angel, hearing his assignment, bends to pick up the arrow and heads for earth.

I "pray-painted" the throne room of heaven, my human imagination struggling to paint a scene impossible to capture on canvas. A few times (really, quite a few times), there was a nudge in my spirit: "No, that is not right." My little block sander, which I use to remove paint from my canvas, received quite a workout.

The finished painting is before you:

Angels portrayed as great and small lights, filling the air.

Angels coming in an endless procession from a side entrance to receive their assignments.

Cherubim, angels who guard the Holiness of God, enveloped in the cloud of smoke at the top of the marble stairs.

*Oh, to be there*—to step through that entrance with the angels—to see the marvels, things unimagined. To touch those majestic curtains, that had become embroidered with fire as I painted them. I would run behind one of the pillars to peer out at the vastness, hardly breathing. Trembling, trusting, overwhelmed by what my eyes beheld, and hoping for an angel to come swiftly to hold me up.

This is what I felt as I sat and immersed myself in the painting. I want to know if you, looking at the painting right now, can see just a little of this glory of heaven. When you watch the angel picking up the arrow, do you sense his gentleness? The one he flies to help will soon feel the brush of his wings. "Are they not all ministering spirits, sent out to render service for the sake of those who will inherit salvation?" (Hebrews 1:14).

~ ~ ~ ~ ~

Clouds of smoke drift high as the Seraphim, the angels above the throne, call out, "Holy, Holy, Holy, is the Lord of hosts, The whole earth is full of His glory" (Isaiah 6:3b). I hope you can hear them.

At the top of the stairs are the Cherubim. Ezekiel describes the scene:

> … a great cloud with fire flashing forth continually … and in its midst something like glowing metal … within it there were figures resembling four living beings. Each of them had four faces … the face of a man … a lion … a bull … an eagle. [They each had] four wings … two touching another being, and two covering their bodies. Now as I looked at the living beings, behold, there was one wheel on the earth beside the living beings, for each of the four of them. The appearance of the wheels and their workmanship was like sparkling beryl … In the midst of the living beings there was something that looked like burning coals of fire, like torches darting back and forth among the living beings. (Ezekiel 1:4-16)

This was an incredible scene to try to capture. Nevertheless, I set myself to work: painting, sanding, and repainting to the edge of despair. It was then that I simply stopped my efforts and said aloud, "I don't know how Father, help me!" At that moment, I realized I had just sent up my first silver arrow prayer. The answer came: "Paint freely; capture the *essence* of these angels, simplicity out of complexity." These words reminded me: "For now we see in a mirror dimly, but then face to face; now I know in part, but then I shall know fully just as I also have been fully known" (1 Corinthians 13:12).

I accept that this painting may not come close to what we will see in heaven. However, since the "No, that is not right" nudges have stopped, it must be close enough to tell the story.

# The Story

My friend Virginia and I were relaxing one evening, talking about the happenings in our lives, when our light conversation turned to the troubling issue of making a living. As with so many in the working world, life responsibilities grow and the emotional and physical strain is very wearing.

Virginia and I prayed, as we have done so often through the years. Pouring out her heart, she said, "Sometimes it is difficult to even turn the knob on the door to enter into another day." How many of us have felt this way? Despite our readiness, the handle is turned, and we step forward.

Virginia's occupation as a caregiver means that she spends each day providing for people who require assistance with the most basic of needs. We prayed that every morning, before she walks into the Group Room, she would remember to send up a "help arrow" prayer, asking the Father to fill her with His compassion and love for those assigned to her. Her desire was that her clients would see Jesus in her eyes, feel Jesus in her touch, hear Jesus in the tone of her voice, and feel His peace fill the room.

As we prayed, a picture of the Lone Ranger with his "silver bullet that never misses its mark," popped into my head. This is how the "help arrow" prayer became a *silver arrow prayer*.

Why is the arrow crumpled? The answer may surprise you. Before it was sent, the little silver arrow prayer had to go through the torture of human thinking:

"I'm sick and tired of this!"

"It won't work."

"I just feel like giving up and walking out."

"Life's too hard."

The brand-new, straight, gleaming silver arrow soon became bent and tarnished. Virginia felt as bent and tarnished as the little arrow. She released a great sigh of relief, when the Holy Spirit brought to her mind the promise of Jesus: "I WILL NEVER DESERT YOU, NOR WILL I EVER FORSAKE YOU" (Heb.13:5b). Against this truth, defeated thinking and the enemy's words fail. When we bring our weariness and doubt to the foot of the cross we are, as always, forgiven and lifted up. Each day now, clutching tightly to His mercy, Virginia bows her head in prayer as she grasps the doorknob. Whether this day will hold a trial or a smile, she knows His provision will be available to her. She lifts her foot in faith to take the first step, then another step, a bolder step. More of Jesus, less of me.

I hope your heart will burn to know the God who bids us to come before His throne. May we grow strong as we learn to lean on Jesus. May all our prayers reach the throne room floor and become solid silver, straight and shining, in His hands.

Remember, when you are in need, the next angel in line can be yours. Send up *your* silver arrow prayer, and feel the rush of wings as he comes swiftly to your aid.

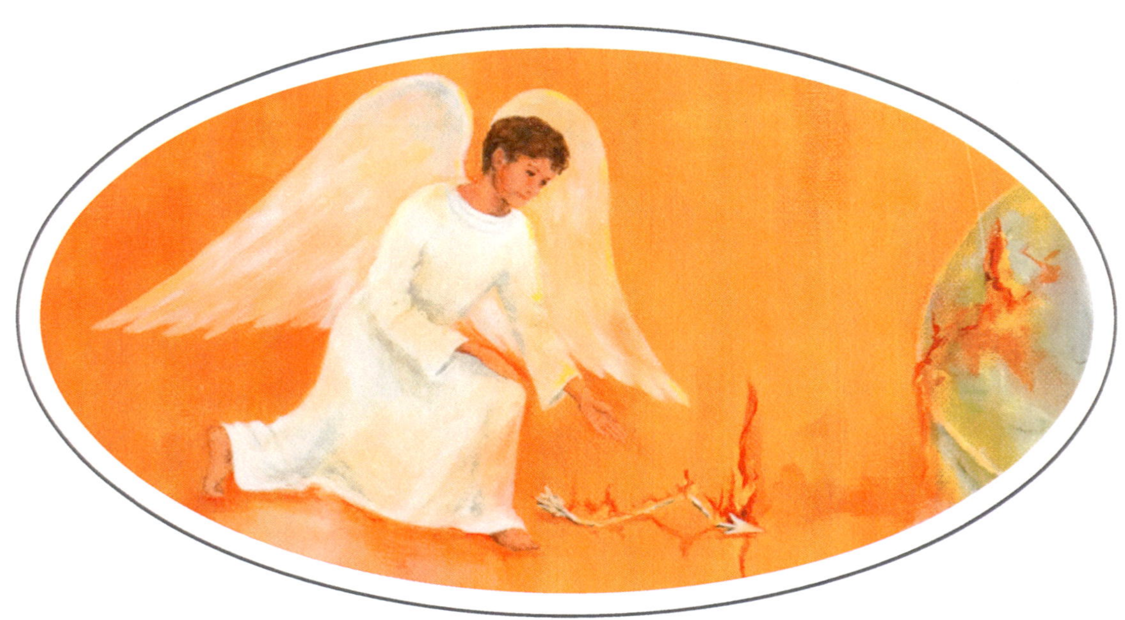

# Gifts of Thorns and a Glass Butterfly

**Thorns** … It was my birthday, and my sister Bonnie held out to me a beautifully wrapped gift. I eagerly took hold of it, but she still held on and we proceeded to have a little tug of war. I laughed, "What is going on?" She said, "I'm not sure you'll like it … it's a little different!" As I opened the box and pushed back the tissue, I was awestruck, for here in my hands lay answered prayer: a crown of thorns. As I blurted this out, Bonnie's eyes grew large and she sat down, saying, "I heard God's heart."

Her tale of this gift starts in a small neighborhood store stocked to the ceiling with unusual wares: her favorite place to seek out treasures. She came upon the crown, and as she picked it up, thoughts of my birthday came, this happened twice, but Bonnie left the store without a purchase. After much back and forth conversation (within herself), she returned for my strange birthday gift, still having doubts.

Why was I praying for a crown of thorns? One of my passions is decorating our church for the different seasons. Spring had arrived and Easter was near. I wanted to place a crown of thorns on our cross as a visual aid, but was at a loss about how to find such an unusual object.

~ ~ ~ ~ ~

Not long after, a close friend came to visit me. Excitedly, I handed her the open box saying, "Look at what my sister gave me." She gently took the crown from its box; it was obvious from the look on her face that her thoughts were far away, she held it for a long while. Later, when I told Bonnie of my friend's touching reaction, the three of us, (the Father, my sister, and me), decided that she would have a crown all her own. The purchase made, the instructions typed and placed inside the box; then carefully wrapped and delivered.

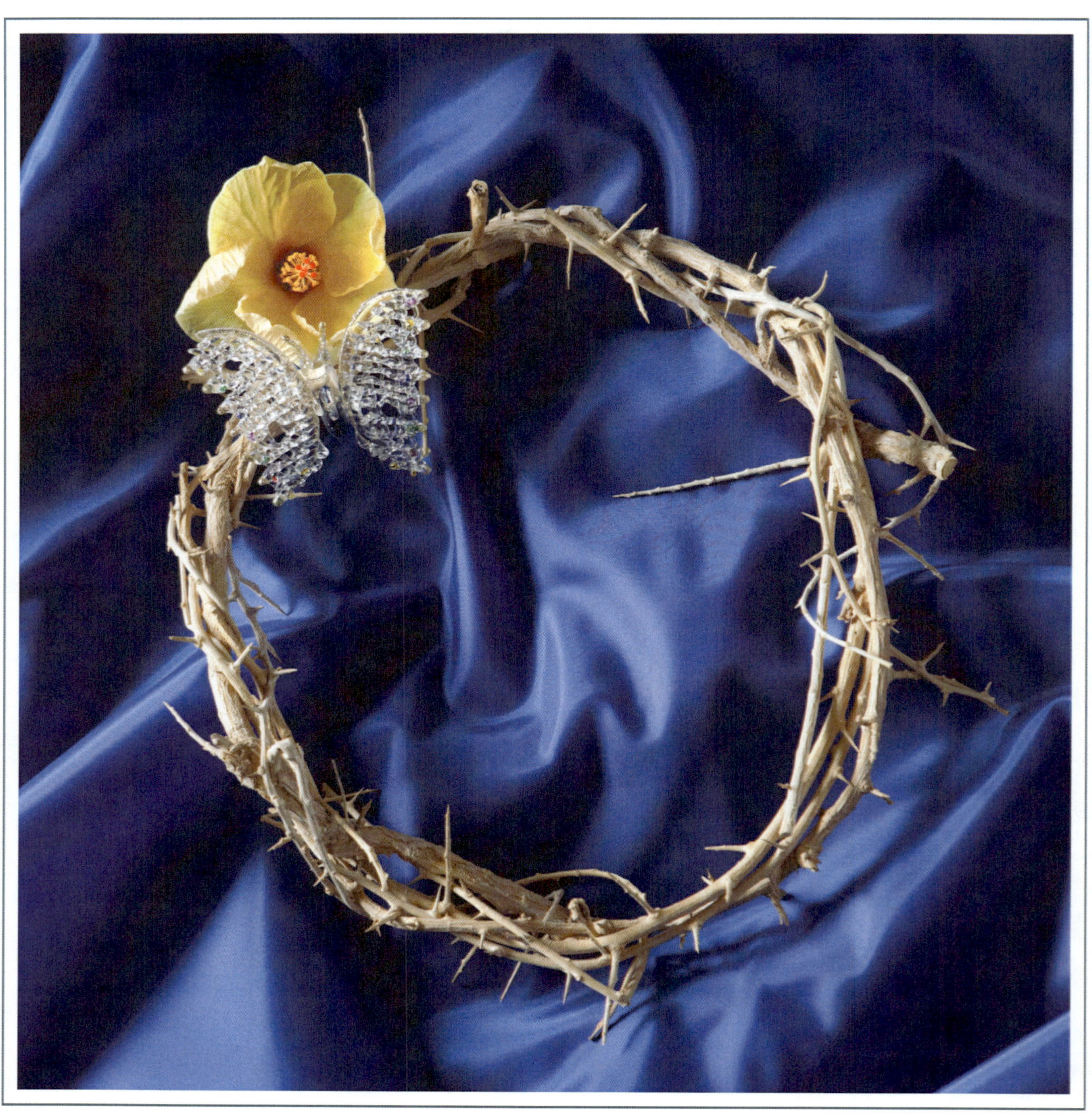

**The instructions read as follows …**

Find a quiet place and sit with Me, Jesus.

Take the crown of thorns into your hands; you will feel the sharpness, just a little.

Take time to listen. Your heart will hear what it so desperately needs. Every person who has ever lived, or will ever live, owns thorns on my crown. Some of the thorns that pierced my brow were for the sins inflicted on you by others, and some of the thorns were sins inflicted by you.

Do not run … stay with me a little longer; do not hide … I know your fear.

I will show you the path of healing and freedom. I walked this path first, at my Father's bidding. It can swallow up any darkness; its name was born in His heart: Forgiveness.

Always remember, this remedy is yours for the asking, all guilt taken away …

> "I acknowledged my sin to Thee,
>
> And my iniquity I did not hide;
>
> I said, "I will confess my transgressions to the Lord";
>
> And Thou didst forgive the guilt of my sin"
>
> (Psalm 32:5).

~ ~ ~ ~ ~

Postscript: I prayed a simple prayer, a request, and the Father took it and used it to touch other lives, I hope you are encouraged to talk with Him as your very best friend, for He is.

~ ~ ~ ~ ~

**and a Glass Butterfly…** It was early December of that same year when my sister walked in the door with a shopping bag full of surprises. A kitchen towel with bright red cherries reminded me of the big cherry tree in our backyard when we were little girls, and the comical sight of our mother trying to scare the hungry birds away, swinging a broom this way and that. She wanted the cherries to bake pies for her daughters.

A pair of cardboard-rimmed glasses with cellophane lenses. When you put them on and looked at a bright light, you saw angel wings! A spun glass ornament, a butterfly; clear glass with beautiful colors all along the outside edges, wings tipped with gold. It brought back long-ago memories of our mother hanging clothes on the line, or leaning forward on her knees weeding the garden. We watched as butterflies would come and light upon her shoulder, or on her hair, how beautiful. Children making memories that, over the years through happy tears make us smile.

I remember it took my breath away as butterflies swarmed into our yard like clouds of moving color. I would wait, very still, until one landed close to me and put its wings together. Then I would move *oh so slowly*—and catch it. Mother warned that if I rubbed the colored powder off their wings, they would not be able to fly. From that point on, I always examined my fingers for specks of color, as if that would help the poor butterfly. I will say all my prisoners happily flew away.

~ ~ ~ ~ ~

Christmas decorating started that year by covering the table in front of my living room window with a blanket of cotton snow. I arranged my collection of Christmas trees to make a small forest, a hand-crocheted star topping every tree. In the center of the table was a wooden angel, lifting a star up to the heavens; my daughter Cathy and I had painted this together. I sprinkled snowflakes over the whole scene, and nestled small-lit candles in the snow, like miniature campfires. It was getting dark outside and snow was starting to fall; the towering evergreens outside became part of my little inside forest.

I turned the lights off and sat down, watching the candle flames flicker. I thanked Him for this miniature scene before me; taking me back to when shepherds stared in awe, while all the stars in heaven and all the trees on earth gave glory to God. The night Jesus was born.

One little white tree in the front seemed to be shouting, "Decorate me!" I remembered the glass butterfly. When I placed it on the tree, I began to think about what else might look nice, maybe something shiny and sparkling to catch the candlelight. I opened my jewelry box and a pin worn at Easter caught my full attention. It was a small gray spike tied with a dark purple ribbon. Too ugly, I thought, but then what happened on Good Friday was ugly. I placed the spike next to the butterfly, hesitant. The little tree was quite satisfied with its two decorations, a butterfly that represents new life, and the ugly gray spike, so we might never forget.

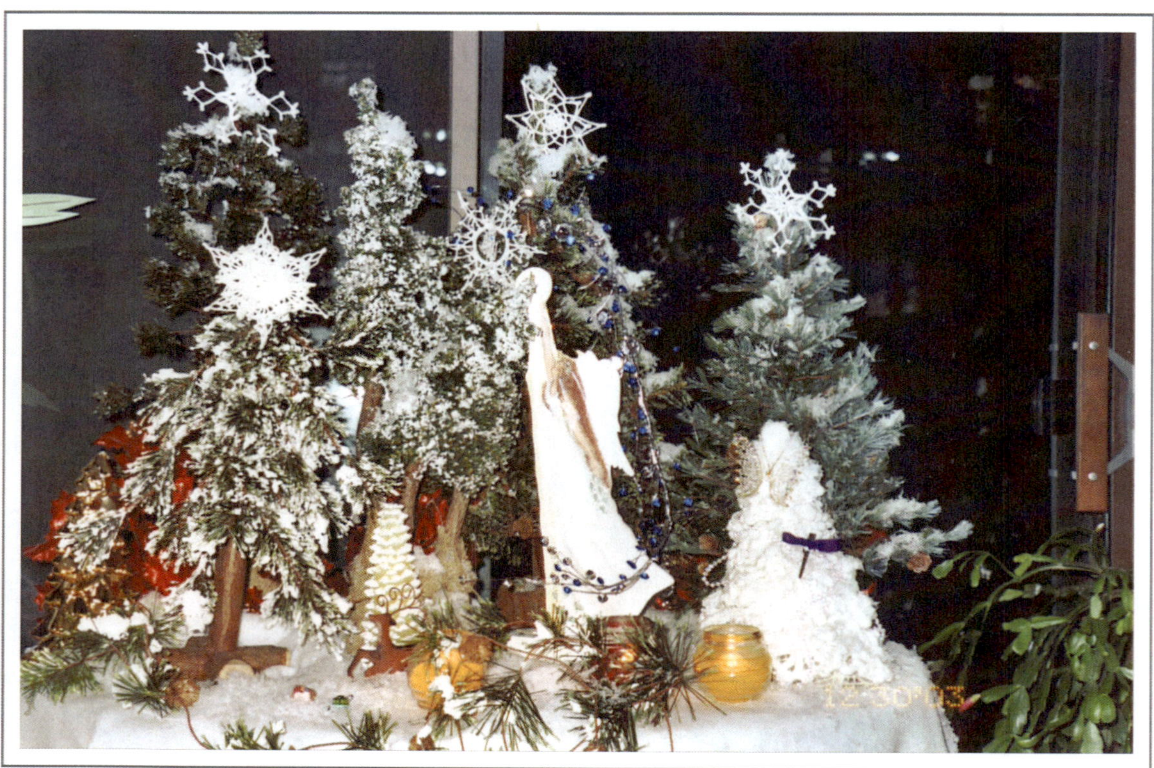

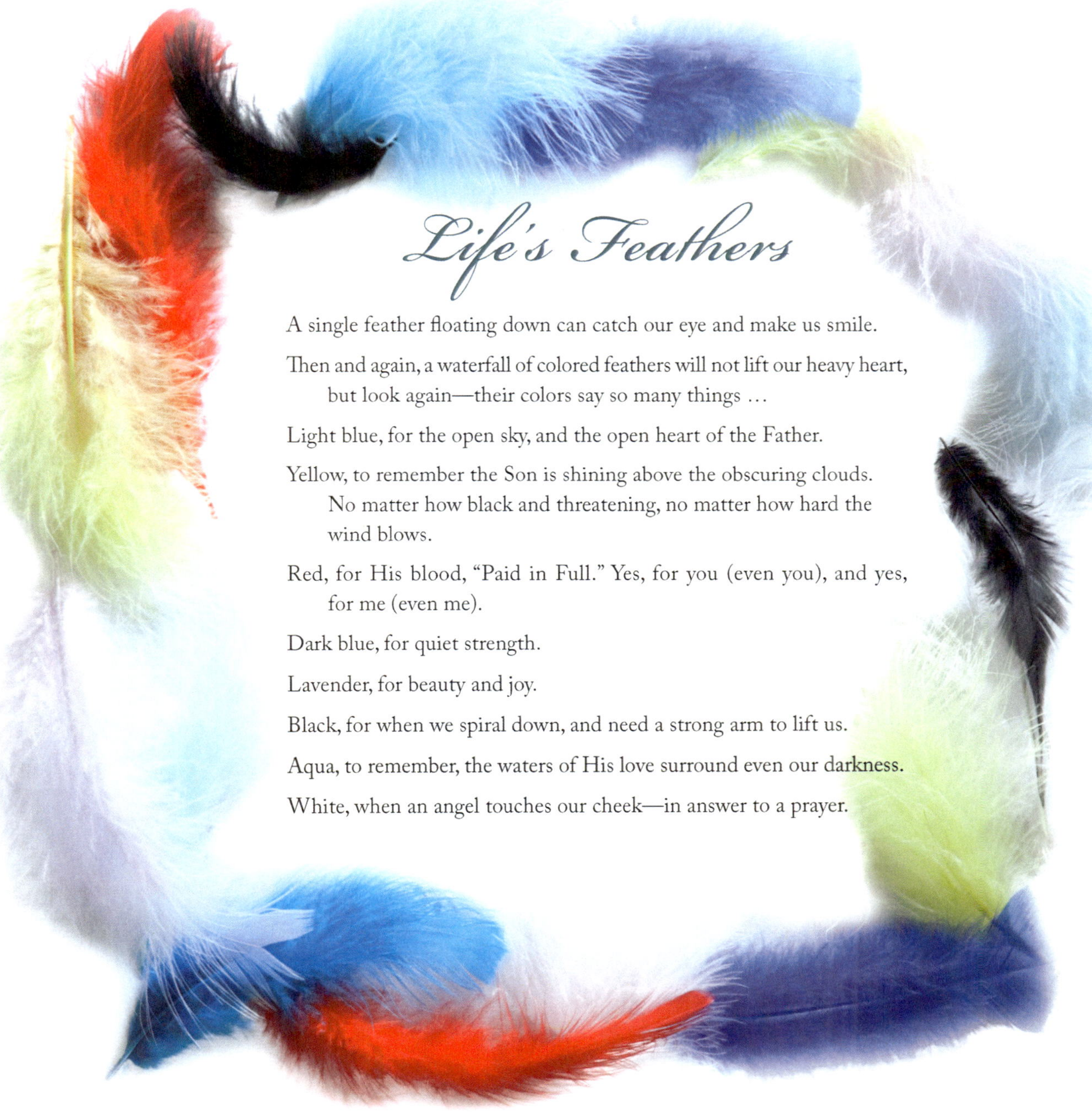



A single feather floating down can catch our eye and make us smile.

Then and again, a waterfall of colored feathers will not lift our heavy heart, but look again—their colors say so many things …

Light blue, for the open sky, and the open heart of the Father.

Yellow, to remember the Son is shining above the obscuring clouds. No matter how black and threatening, no matter how hard the wind blows.

Red, for His blood, "Paid in Full." Yes, for you (even you), and yes, for me (even me).

Dark blue, for quiet strength.

Lavender, for beauty and joy.

Black, for when we spiral down, and need a strong arm to lift us.

Aqua, to remember, the waters of His love surround even our darkness.

White, when an angel touches our cheek—in answer to a prayer.

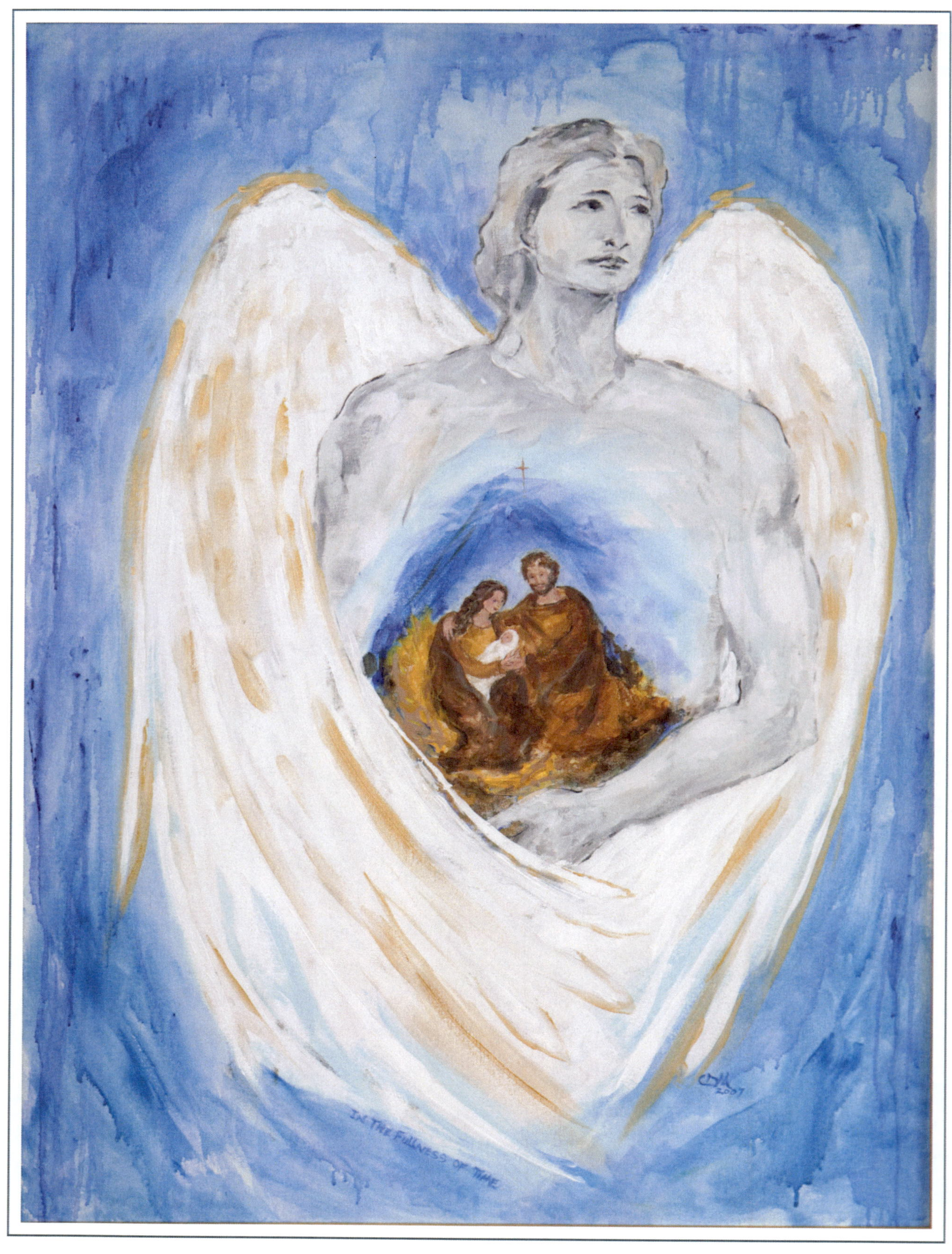

IN THE FULLNESS OF TIME

# Tears

## The Painting

As if scooped up from the earth, Joseph, Mary and her newborn—held close against the strong chest of a heavenly being. Joseph's arm comes around Mary, reassuring her, as they are far from home in a strange crude shelter. Crude yes, but the heat from the animals is warm and comforting, the soft lowing soon has the infant asleep. Unseen, gigantic wings give covering from the sudden downpour. The angel keeps one hand on his sword, as there is much danger. His name is Guardian.

## The Story

It is beginning to rain, and as Guardian looks up, he realizes the drops are not rain—they are tears. The tears of heaven's angels are falling; the birth of Jesus has taken place on earth, but He is sorely missed in heaven. Guardian looks towards his fellows: "What does it mean that the Son of God has come down to the world of men?"

They watch as a lone angel announces the birth of Jesus to a group of very frightened shepherds. "And the angel said to them, 'Do not be afraid; for behold, I bring you good news of a great joy which shall be for all the people; for today in the city of David there has been born for you a Savior, who is Christ the Lord. And this will be a sign for you: you will find a baby wrapped in cloths, and lying in a manger'" (Luke 2: 10-12).

The angels' tears become exploding rockets of praise, lighting up the sky: "And suddenly there appeared with the angel a multitude of the heavenly host praising God, and saying, 'Glory to God in the highest, And on earth, peace among men with whom He is pleased'" (Luke 2:13-14). Guardian looks down at his small charge, and tries to imagine what the future will hold.

The years of maturing are accomplished, Guardian always by His side. Jesus has now reached the age to start the work His Father has given Him. He chooses twelve men for companions and begins to teach them, answering their many questions, capturing their thoughts, correcting—all this as they walk the dusty roads.

When evening approaches they make camp, and their bond of friendship strengthens as they sit round the fire eating; their laughter rings out over the darkening green hills. These are wonderful nights, lying on sweet-smelling grass and looking at stars through the branches of olive trees. Jesus telling them marvels. Guardian watches, and listens.

For three years the crowds have come. Jesus, filled with compassion heals them. Blind eyes see, lepers made whole, and tormenting demons are cast-out. When they become hungry, Jesus feeds them with bread, and His words feed their souls with truth. At nightfall, when His human body feels crushed and earthly emotions are stretched beyond limit, the need to commune with His Father overtakes Him. Into the quiet of the mountain, He goes to pray. Guardian is still with Him.

Then Guardian receives new orders: Do nothing to stop the events that are soon to take place, and to hold back his protection. He will obey, but again he wonders, "What does this mean?" Too soon, he will know.

Other angels come to watch with Guardian. It is hard for them to witness as the very people Jesus came to save, turn Him over to the Roman authorities with their lies. He is beaten, spit upon; then the loud cry, "Crucify Him!" (Mark 15:14b). Tears stream down the faces of the angels, hands at their sides—helpless.

Then the nails … Oh, the nails.

The wooden cross is lifted high; they are filled with anguish.

The angels look at the people gathered around the cross. Some have faces distorted with jeering, others, ashen with grief. A last breath and Jesus is dead. Their tears cease with shock; there is no understanding, only sorrow.

Guardian stays with the body—a painful, solitary privilege. He keeps his vigil feeling as cold as the tomb; but his heart burns with questions. Friday afternoon (oh so slowly) becomes Sunday morning.

Then, the dark tomb *fills with life*—**Jesus rises** from the dead. Guardian is overwhelmed; tears of joy flood his being and he almost flings his arms around Jesus. Instead, he comes to attention, resuming his post. His questions answered, "and know that this One is indeed the Savior of the world" (John 4:42b). Guardian has been granted the honor, to look into the way of man's salvation, "– things into which angels long to look" (1 Peter 1:12b).

~ ~ ~ ~ ~

If *your* life is as a shadow filled tomb … roll the stone from your heart's entrance and welcome Jesus in. The clean, fresh, wind of His promises will soon blow the webs of despair to nothing.

# He Stands at the Door

## The Painting

I chose my whitest white; purple, mauve, blue, red, yellow, and gold; colors to try to express holiness, power, and beauty. I hunkered down near the canvas, painting with fast strokes the power coming from His hands. When I stood back, I was amazed at what He had done with my paintbrush, and (I was having so much fun painting!)

Simple lines depict the doorway, the day is coming when the Father will say, "Son, it is time to bring our family home!"

I was impressed to paint the words, FOR YOU, the Y as a sculptured, gold communion cup … filled with love, and Jesus sacrifice.

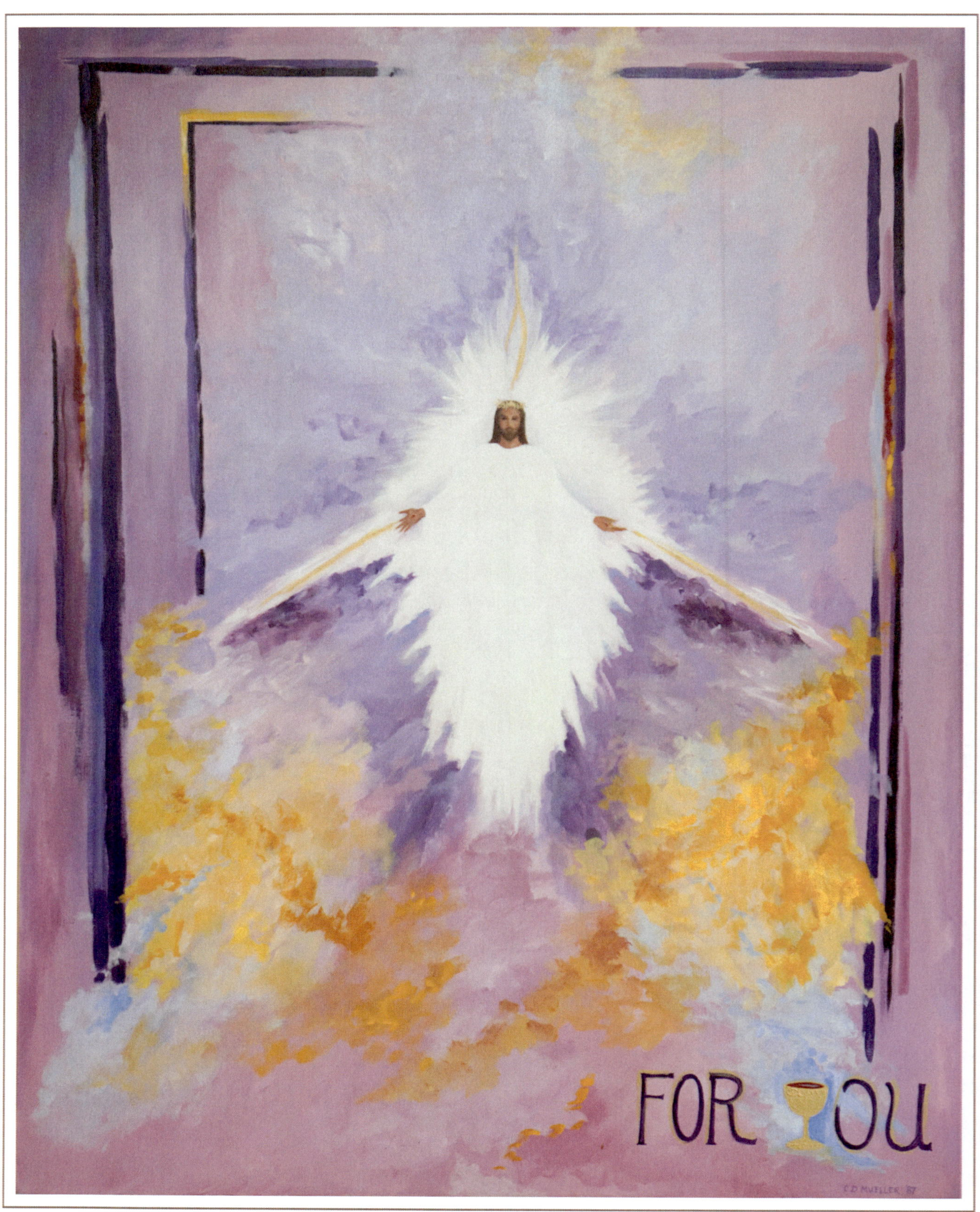


FOR YOU

"For the Lord Himself will
descend from heaven with a shout,
with the voice of the archangel,
and with the trumpet of God;
and the dead in Christ shall rise first.

Then we who are alive
and remain shall be caught up
together with them in the clouds
to meet the Lord in the air, and
thus we shall always be with the Lord.
Therefore comfort one another
with these words"
(1 Thessalonians 4:16-18).

"… knowing that you were not
redeemed with perishable things
like silver or gold from your futile
way of life inherited from
your forefathers, but with
precious blood,
as of a lamb unblemished and
spotless, the blood of Christ"
(1 Peter 1:18-19).

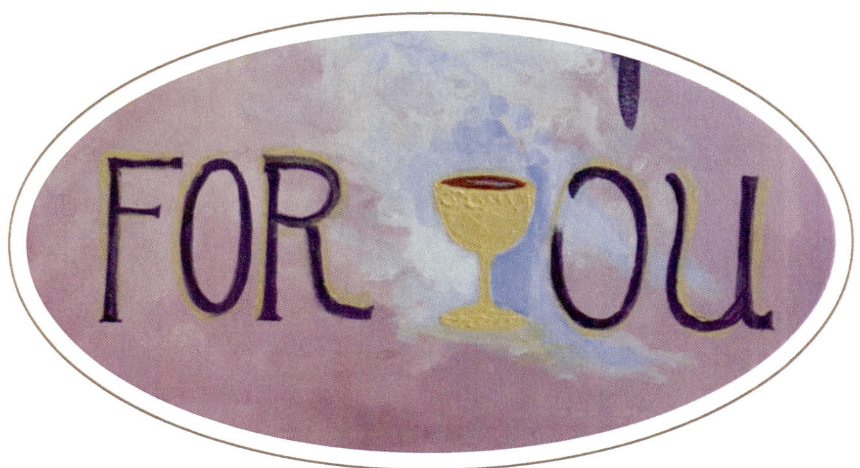

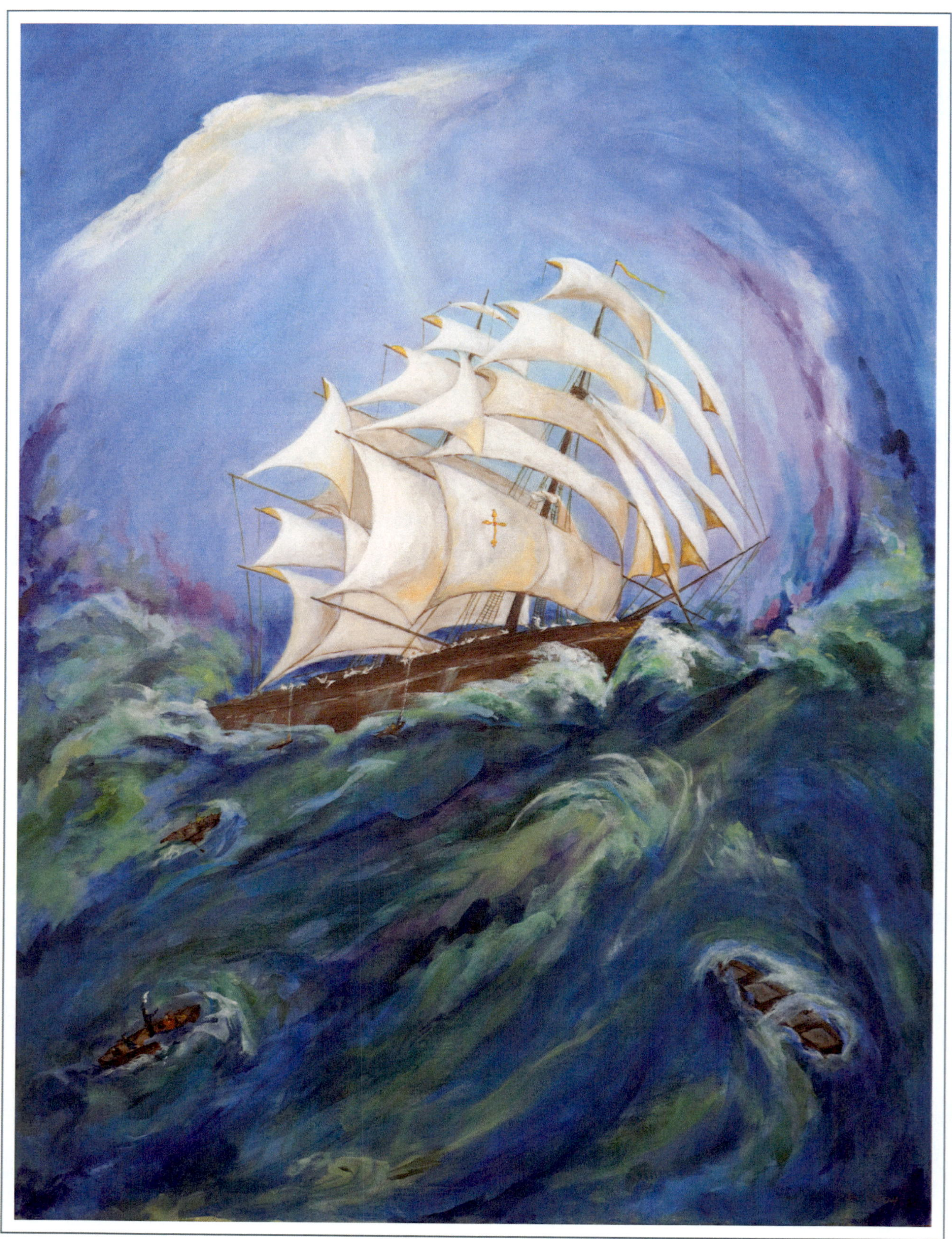

# A Call to Purpose

One Sunday morning, during a pause in the worship, a deacon of my church was moved by the Holy Spirit to speak to us. He shared the vision of our church as an embattled ship, sails full in the wind, a cross emblazoned on the mainsail. It steers through angry waters amid threats of disaster, driven on its rescue mission by Christ's love for a sea of lost souls. As he spoke, his words became alive in my mind. I went home and started to paint.

## The Painting

The clipper ship represents the Church of Jesus Christ—each church, perhaps, its own ship—or the ship as Christ's Church, entire. All the people on board are dressed in white, a sign that they belong to Jesus. The ship is surrounded by a violent storm; waves swelling high lift the ship, and then heaves it low. Rising from the sea, a terrible serpent heads for the ship's bow—waiting for the opportunity to strike … the enemy never sleeps. The longboats are hard-pressed to reach the ship as the waves of the world vie for the souls of men.

There is, however, a protective calm directly around the ship. The Father is watching over the rescuers, His guiding light shining down through a bright tear in the wind-tossed sky. Two of the longboats reach the ship; rope ladders drop over the railing, and hails go out to encourage the exhausted survivors.

In the remaining longboats, the reactions vary. There is a family in one boat. The husband bravely stands, waving his kerchief and pleading through the wind, "Rescue us!" Others sit crouched in fear; they will have to be snatched from peril by a willing soul, someone who will risk his or her own life to climb over the railing and down a moving ladder to grab hold of them. In another boat there are those who ignore the hope extended; they are listening only to the lies told by their pride- shaped hearts. Each voices the same reply: "I don't need You!" Jesus, even now, bids them to come.

Sadly, in the corner, an empty longboat; the waves seem to have captured it. As I look, my heart feels heavy—and empty at the same time. I sink below the waters with it. This boat represents the lost. Who were these people? Was there no one to help them? Its emptiness is as profound as eternity.

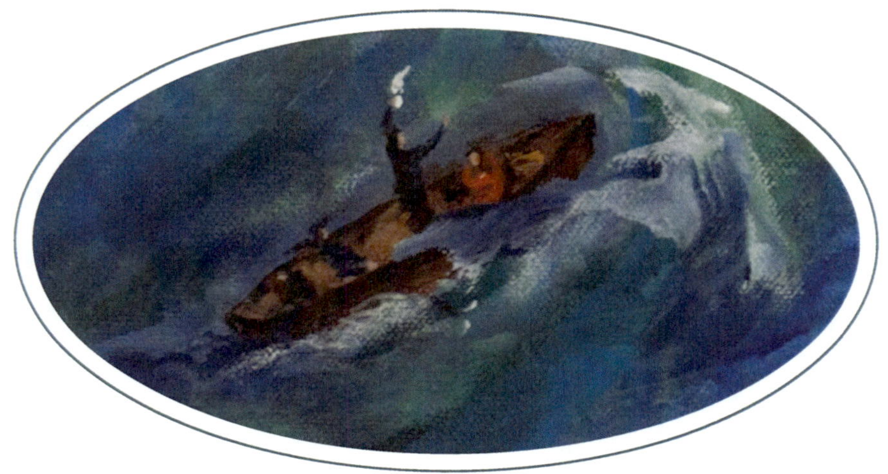

# The Call

The message of this painting is both personal, and a call to the church. "Follow Me, and I will make you fishers of men" (Matt.4:19).

To be a fisher of men—to keep His truth and, as He leads, to offer salvation; this is the greatest of privileges. My own rod, reel, and bait are made of words, paint, and paintbrushes. At this very moment, men and women the world over are on their knees, fashioning beautiful fishing flies of prayer. This prayer will be a covering for those who have put on wading boots and are going out into the deep waters of life. In heaven there is a storehouse filled with fishing rods of hope, nets of kindness, and tackle boxes filled with love. Jesus is tending the pick-up window today. Your fishing gear is ready. It is just a prayer away.

~ ~ ~ ~ ~

A thought occurs to me. Are *you* in one of the longboats, waiting for rescue? Your heart may now understand a little of who this Jesus is. Here, take my hand ….

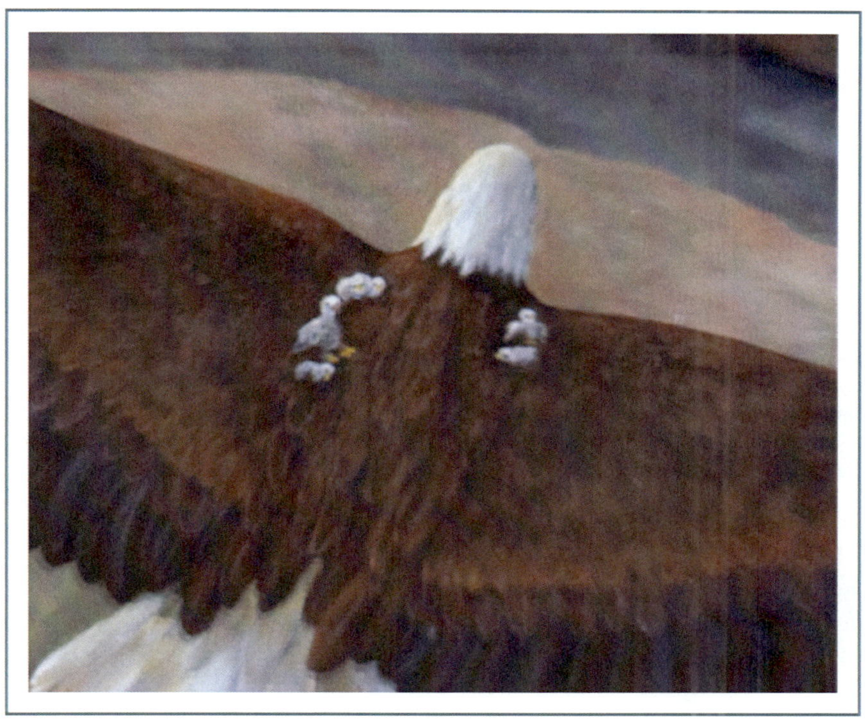

# Tell Me about the Mountain

## The Paintings

A great eagle pushes off from his post. The watch is his now. Ever vigilant, he circles the sanctuary. He is a Watchman.

"And Abraham called the name of that place The Lord Will Provide, as it is said to this day, 'In the mount of the Lord it will be provided'" (Genesis 22: 14).

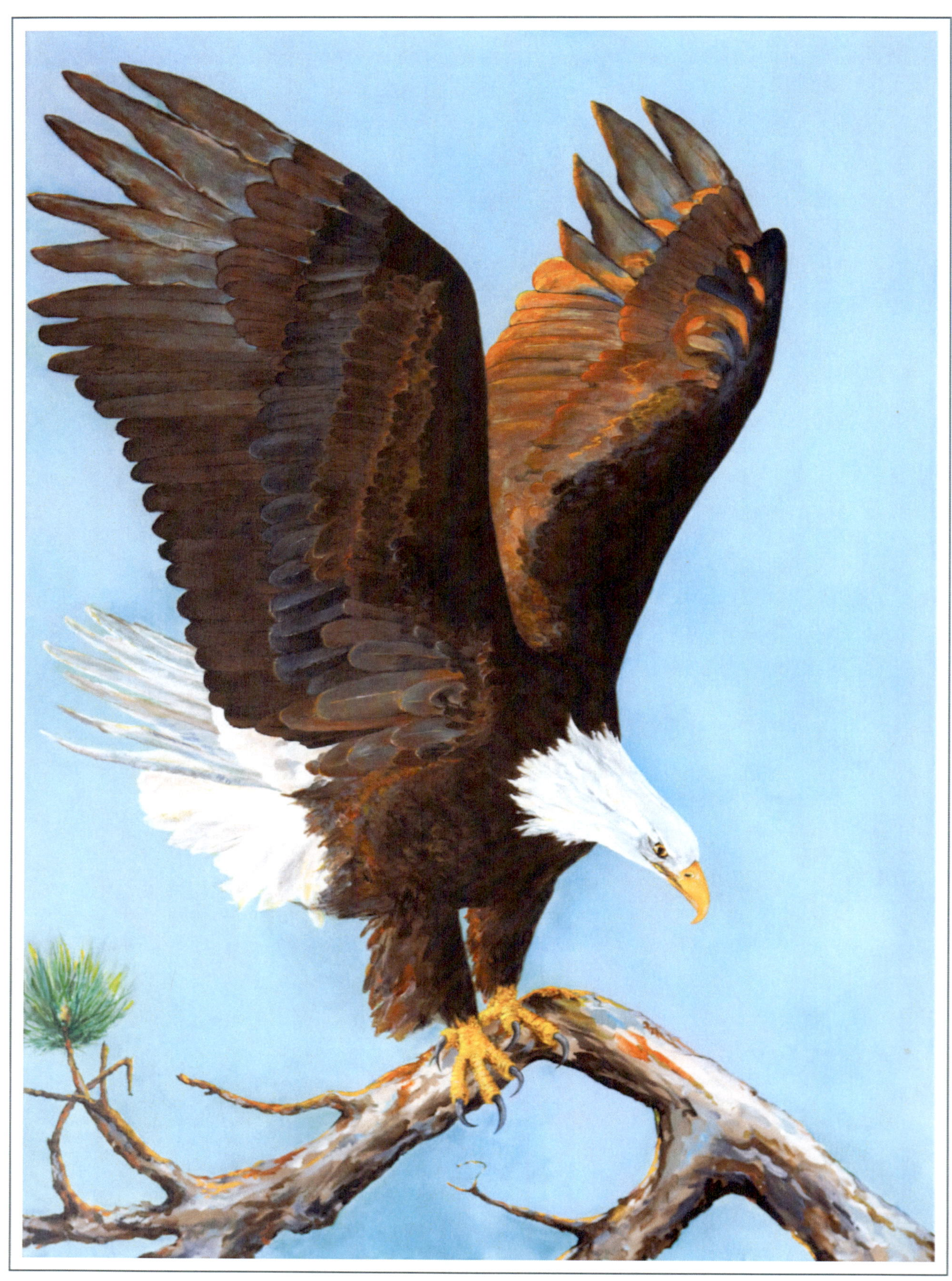

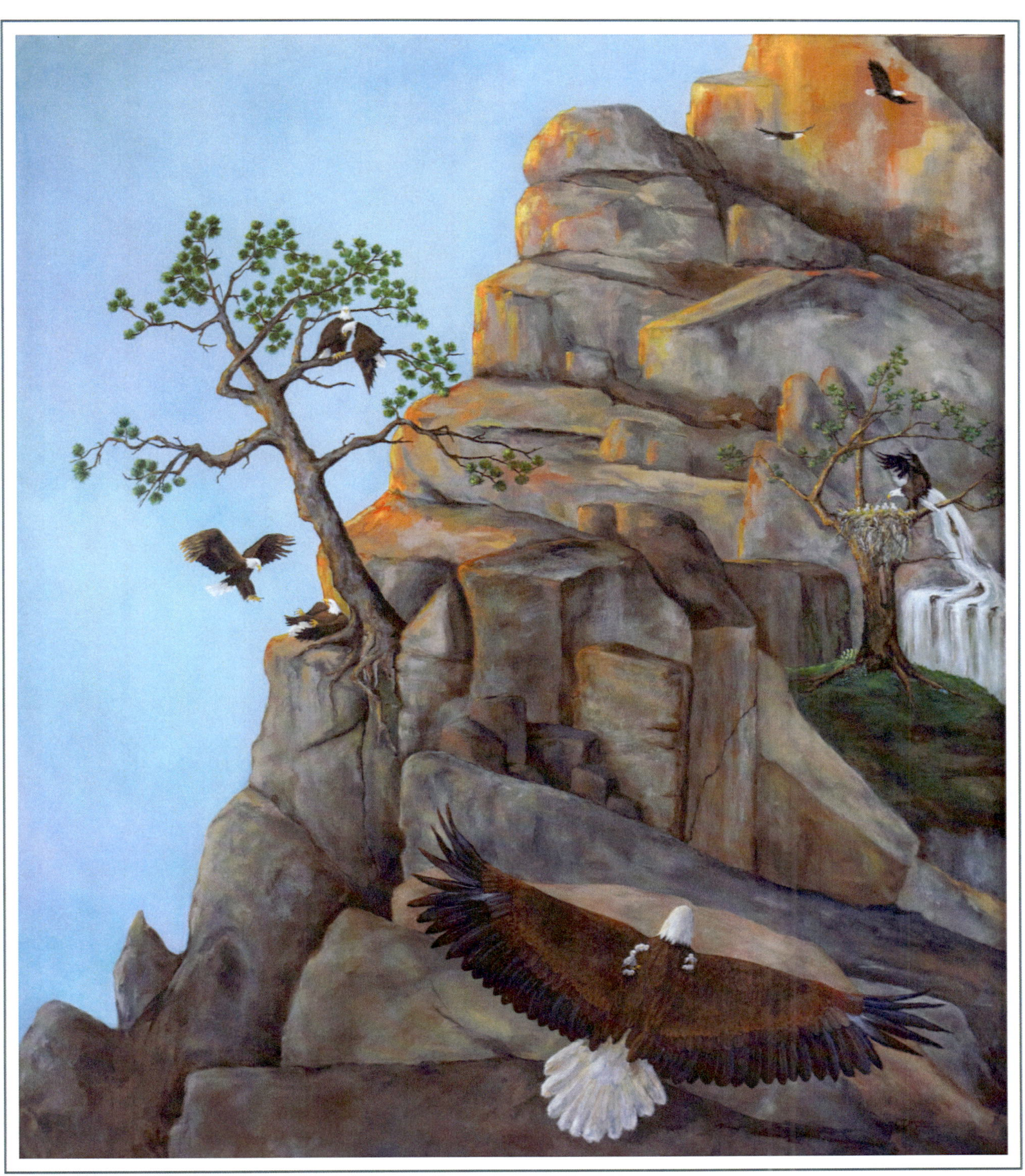

As the sun sets on this rugged fortress, rocks turn to gold. Two eagles soar above, high and free, of one mind and one purpose: *to fly into the love of the Father.*

A lone tree juts into the sky; winds and the many landings of eagles have scarred it with broken limbs and bare places. Determined roots grow out from the rock, exposed to the elements. Storms have pulled and rain has threatened, but it ever stands. Despite intense adversity, its clusters of needles are green with life, and the new shoots point up like candles of hope. This tree will hold. It is the Healing Tree on the mountain of God.

On one bough, an eagle with a broken wing rests painfully on the breast of a friend, and is comforted. At the foot of the tree lies a new arrival, too wounded to fly; exhaustion and fear grip her. She extends her talons to protect herself, resisting her rescuer who hovers above bringing food and hope. He sees her distress and leaves for the moment, planning to return after God's peace has done its work.

Too numerous to count are those who have leaned against this tree. They come, physically broken, no longer able to ascend with the wind. There are ones so weary and shattered in spirit, with wounds too deep to bleed; ones who only the secret knowledge of God can repair.

*This tree represents the heart of God,*

*His arm gathering them into Himself.*

The sun warms the old nest, cradled in the ancient pine tree. Little ones reach up with open beaks to the mothering eagle that tends to their needs. A nearby waterfall sings a lullaby, and the fragrance of flowers fills the air. Here on the mountain is an oasis, complete with soft grass—just in case an eaglet should topple from the nest. The cruel memories these tender young orphans carry will soon fade away in this beautiful safe place. In time, they will grow strong wings and leave the nest. Some will go back into the world, seeking the hurting and lost; others will begin training as Watchmen on God's holy mountain.

*This tree represents the hand of God …*

*Provision for the helpless.*

In the foreground, an eagle starts his descent to the nest; his charges nestled on his back in protective feathers. He carries them out of harm's way on strong wings.

# The Laughter of the Enemy and God's Stubborn Love

This is a story of the hidden shadows of a mind—my mind. If you will come with me, I will tell you of the power of God's stubborn love in overcoming the cruelty and laughter of the enemy. With those who have chosen to walk the life-road with Jesus, (as well as those who are very close to taking their first step), I would like to share the tools and comforts He has given to me. For although our paths may be quite different, one thing is certain; we need to help each other on our way, praising God together.

Jesus watched as His plan for my life unfolded. He watched as I struggled, and did not step in to take the pain away when I fell. As we do not help a baby bird escape from its shell, or a butterfly out of its chrysalis; He knew that the struggle made my wings stronger. My early wings were very weak, and I often failed to trust and believe. The slightest wind of adversity and I would fall to the ground, defeated. He always picked me up, gently placed me back in the nest, and let me continue to struggle.

The enemy—my enemy, your enemy—used unbelief as his main weapon. Knowing this, Jesus gave me the tenacity to seek Him. Many times my prayer was only a weak call of His name, only a whisper. I did not think heaven heard me, but not only did heaven hear, the enemy heard—and fled. *Jesus*, the name above all names, a perfect prayer.

My journey started as a young teen at a little neighborhood church. They were having a Vacation Bible School, and one afternoon a teacher took me aside and quietly inquired if I had asked Jesus to come into my heart. I said "no." She asked if I would like her to pray with me. I answered "yes," but as she started praying, I put up a mental wall, blocking that prayer from touching me. Inside, my thoughts were, "Not now, not now, some day, some year in the future I'll give my life to you." Jesus heard my "some day."

Even at my young age, I understood that prayer to be a commitment, and I have never forgotten the words she prayed. They came back to me repeatedly, as the years flew by and life became busier. I chose to live my life without God; I did not allow my conscience to consider God's will, but only what I thought was good or bad. "There is a way which seems right to a man, But its end is the way of death" (Proverbs

14: 12). I was in great danger. In His mercy, Jesus held on and worked in my life.

It was a simple task, to take dirty clothes to a Laundromat, fill the machines, put the coins in, then push "start" and wait. I walked around, perused the bulletin board, and stared out the window at the passing cars. I was checking my machines for the umpteenth time when I spied a small booklet on one of the folding tables. It was the book of Proverbs. Printed on the cover was, "For as he thinks within himself, so he is" (Proverbs 23:7a). That sentence gripped me and would not let go … I knew my thoughts. I left that Laundromat with clean clothes and the unsettling realization that I was dirty.

I sat on my bed and talked to Jesus for a long time, and then I spoke one word, "yes." It was enough, with the core of that long ago-prayer ingrained on my heart. When I enter heaven, I would like to thank the person who obeyed Jesus and left that little booklet for me to find.

For those who have never heard the Sinner's Prayer, and for those who have been in hiding from Him:

Heavenly Father, I confess I am a sinner; I am in need of your forgiveness. Jesus, I believe you suffered in my place on the cross. I believe you died to pay the full cost of my sin, and on the third day rose from the grave. Father, to say that I am sorry, is so small, but it is all I have to bring. I now ask that you take me in, forgive me, and make me your own. I humbly ask this, in Jesus's name, Amen.

That night I slept soundly, but in my waking moments, the enemy gave me a swift jab: "Do you really believe that prayer meant anything?" A little dumbfounded, I stumbled out of bed and tried to go about my morning routine, coffee and reading. The enemy's words were swirling into every corner of my mind, looking for a permanent home. The book I was reading was one of a science fiction series I had been following for quite a while. The author had started to interject foul language and sex, but I kept on reading the series, glossing over those unwelcome portions. As I settled in to read on that life-changing morning, I heard a definite "No!" I kept reading. "No!" This time I answered back: "I'm not reading the bad parts!" Back and forth, back and forth, finally, I gave up and put the book down. I finished my coffee, collected the paperbacks, and (literally) destroyed the whole series. End of argument. I was made strongly aware of the fact that there is no glossing over evil. Now, I think back on that encounter with the Holy Spirit and laugh a little, imagining both of us facing each other with our hands on our hips. I was stubborn, the Holy Spirit patient, and I am forever grateful.

My walk as a Christian did not start out as a honeymoon, in the way I have heard many tell their stories. Mine was a walk filled with fiery darts of doubt and ugly, appalling thoughts. At the time, I took these thoughts as mine. I was so wrong. I lived through each day waiting for evening; I searched myself to sense Jesus's comforting presence. Finding Him, I would sigh with relief. Then I would start to question Him: "How can I be Yours with all these wicked thoughts inside of me?" Pleading, "Please, take them away." As the weeks and months went by, the bombardment continued. My belief was shaken, but still I clung to Him.

Into my distressed life came a much-needed friend, Lois. She watched over me like a mother hen, clucking and pecking, in human terms, just plain straight talking and praying. A group of women met once a week at her home to pray, and I often called them from work, my voice crying for help: "I need prayer." I had thirty-five minutes for lunch break; it was a literal race for me to punch out, drive, pray, drive, and punch back in. They waited at the door for me—praying. They told me repeatedly, "It is not *you* thinking these thoughts. It is the enemy." I did not believe them. I held to the idea that it was evil me, and the enemy laughed.

One evening I reached inside myself and felt emptiness. "Jesus, where are you!" All strength drained from my body and terror filled me, like a mother who has lost sight of her child. The light inside me was gone. I stood as if in a dark cave, my fingers groping against cold stone, my heart confused. I lived in this cave, day after day, searching to escape. I did not understand that the tight grip of Jesus was holding me, guiding me.

I received an invitation to hear a pastor speak about his missionary work in Africa. He told story after story of demon forces and their defeat, bodies healed, and minds set free by Jesus. I thought of calling him, to spill out my torment and to have him pray for me. It was five agonizing months later that I made an appointment to talk with him. On the long drive to his church, I remember thinking maybe, just maybe, he would have the answer for me. He listened as I emptied my heart, then asked if I would like to do a prayer exercise together. The first step was to explain to God exactly how I felt about everything that had been happening in my life, holding nothing back. I did just that (while using half a box of tissues). Then we asked for the Father's guidance, protection, and the infilling of the Holy Spirit, all in the name of Jesus. I learned something wonderful that day. The Holy Spirit knows the intricate details of our lives, and no human emotion or circumstance surprises Him. He stays with us in the locked prisons of our minds. In loneliness—our hearts hurting so that we fall to the floor in pain—He rocks us in His arms. I also learned that He does not leave when we slip and fall into sin, nor does He condemn us. His love leads us to repentance.

Reverend Jim and I opened our Bibles. He suggested that each of us read quietly until a verse "jumped up from the page." I looked at him a little oddly when he made that statement, but followed his instructions. It happened! I wrote my verse down, word for word; Pastor Jim wrote his as well. Now, we would listen for Jesus to speak to our hearts. The Bible tells us, "To him the doorkeeper opens, and the sheep hear his voice, and he calls his own sheep by name, and leads them out" (John 10:3).

I kept Pastor Jim's notes; the scripture, and the words he heard for me:

*"And the God of peace will soon crush Satan under your feet.*

*The grace of our Lord Jesus be with you" (Romans 16: 20).*

*"Jim, Charlene needs My peace of heart, a peace that sustains her even in the midst of Satanic and sinful manifestations in her mind and this will come. She needs to let Me become Lord of her mind, of her thinking. This can only be done by deliberately taking time day by day in meditation and prayer. She needs to "see" Satan being crushed under MY feet, along with her bad thoughts. That is a place to start. As she learns to come to Me like this, day by day, submitting her mind to Me, letting her mind actually think My thoughts, she will find that eventually her mind will become more and more free of Satanic and sinful control."*

The answer was clear; I was to start stocking the shelves of my mind with scripture, and let His words crowd out the enemy. Reverend Jim emphasized that as I continued to do this prayer exercise at home, to keep in mind that if what I wrote down did not line up with God's Word, scratch it from the page. Finally, we turned everything into a prayer, with many thanks.

Peace filled my whole being as I drove home. I wrote Reverend Jim, thanking him for his help.


Most mornings now, I wake up with coffee and the Word of God, praying and listening. I found my journal from just after my visit with Reverend Jim. I had written, "I'm scared, I'm afraid you won't be there, or I won't hear you, but I'm going to trust you." Then I listened for His voice. "Dear Charlene (the "dear" was emphasized), I love you." Oh, how my heart soared.

I was now on a roller-coaster ride, way up, and then way down. As Jesus kept shining His light on truth, small victories started taking place in my mind. The storm clouds parted and sunlight seeped into my dark, hidden places, exposing them.

Now my cave wasn't as dark. I was able to see the tools He had left for me: a large pane of glass propped up against the cave wall and on the floor next to it, a thick black marker and one army boot. I stood there wondering what I was to do next. Ahhh … I picked up the marker and wrote UNBELIEF in huge letters on the glass pane. I put on the army boot, and crashed through the glass. A battle won! For a while, there was a spring in my step.

At a snail's pace and without me even realizing it, the darkness returned. The war was not over. I saw the enemy's fiery darts coming toward me and felt the sting of them hitting their mark—me. I cowered in a niche of my cave, peering around to see if I could make a run for it. There was something blocking my escape: gigantic letters spelling DOUBT and UNBELIEF. I groaned. My heart became cold, almost slowing to a stop; I felt defeated. Then, like a fire taking hold, my heart grew warm and beat loudly in my ears, and I heard His words: "Climb over, dig under, squeeze through, don't stop, keep moving!" I climbed, I dug, I did not stop. Not by my strength, but by the strength of Jesus, another battle won.

Moving through the cave, I discover yet another tool, a gift: the "Invisible Garbage Can." I have come across so many who battle in this mind-war, and I relish sharing this gift. It is always the same, eyes filled with pain come alive with hope. This remarkable garbage can looks just like the kind that can be purchased at any hardware store, sort of grayed-silver in color, even dented in a few places. However, when you lift the lid of this garbage can, all you see is an empty tube going into blackness. Let me explain. When you use the drive-up window at a bank, you put your deposit in a tube and *whoosh*, it goes straight to the teller. Then it comes back to you. The design of this garbage can sends deposits straight to Hell. Yes, you read correctly. There is no return whoosh; it is a *one-way* trip. Feel free to deposit any thought that does not line up with the Word of God: prideful, evil, or self-condemning. In other words, the thoughts of the enemy—those words that he loves to whisper in our ear. Once you have asked the Father for your personal garbage can, it stays at your side. We are, after all, a work in progress.

## DIRECTIONS for the use of the "INVISIBLE GARBAGE CAN"

~ Alarm! An enemy thought has entered. On Guard!

~ Reach up and quickly take a tight hold on the unwanted thought.

    (If in public, pretend you are putting a stray hair back in place).

~ Speak aloud (if possible) the scripture verses you have committed to memory. My favorite is:

    "We are destroying speculations and every lofty thing raised up against the knowledge of God, and we are taking every thought captive to the obedience of Christ" (2 Corinthians 10:5).

~ Lift the lid. (If in public, this is easily disguised by a multitude of actions).

~ Give the thought a shove down the tube, and replace the lid.

~ Repeat as often as necessary. It may be a thousand time a day, do not give up.

~ Take a moment or two to come close to Jesus, and give Him your brightest smile.

Remember, every *whoosh* is another battle won. I have used a little humor in this list of directions, but remember, the enemy is serious and waits for our destruction. Now for some good news: the reward of diligence is a renewed mind. Be faithful. Jesus is. "And faithfulness the belt about His waist" (Isaiah 11:5b).

All I have related to you went on for over a year. I was tired. I had turned to Jesus with all my might, but the torturous thoughts overcame. With my last strength, I called Lois and thankfully heard that the prayer group was meeting. I drove there at lunch-break, and they tenderly prayed for me. As I walked slowly down the driveway to return to work, they called after me: "Remember, His wings are covering you." I heard, but I was numb. I returned to work, and sat at my desk unable to function. I was afraid and could do nothing to help myself.

Suddenly, all the weight of my struggles literally lifted off my shoulders. As it lifted, I pictured the weight as that of the bulky shoulder pads on an exhausted football player, or the heavy yoke and harness of a workhorse. My mind was clear. I was able to breathe; I was free. These words filled my heart:

> *Just hold onto the facts that I know deep down are true and I am searching to feel, but the feelings will not come on purpose, because that is where faith has to step in and must take over. When Satan is allowed to come at you and God watches, faith in Jesus must win.*

Remember how I pleaded, "Please take these thoughts away." I received my answer about six months later. "Because you would have left Me, and gone back into the world." Jesus used the enemy's tactics to defeat the enemy. For as long as I was being tormented, my mind chased after Jesus. Even when I thought He would reject me, I continued to call out for Him.

You would think that after so many skirmishes, I would be wise to the enemy's actions. Too often, I failed, and still fail, to remember the past rescues of my Savior, and worse, not wearing my armor.

Put on the full armor of God, that you may be able to stand firm against the schemes of the devil. Stand firm therefore, HAVING GIRDED YOUR LOINS WITH TRUTH, and HAVING PUT ON THE BREAST-PLATE OF RIGHTEOUSNESS, and having shod YOUR FEET WITH THE PREPARATION OF THE GOSPEL OF PEACE ... taking up the shield of faith … take the HELMET OF SALVATION, and the sword of the Spirit, which is the word of God … pray. (Ephesians 6:11, 14-18)

When I began writing this part of my story, Fear raised its foul head; I recoiled, sinking into a deep fog. I curled up on my couch, eyes fixed on the television, stuffing myself with food. Depression made his entrance and, like superglue, kept me from wanting to move. A friend recognized I was in trouble and prayed. I was again, rescued.

Recently a new help has arrived, the word "no." A very small word, but power-packed. I am sure my neighbors (I live in a condominium) wonder, when, out of the blue and at almost any time of the day or night, they hear a loud, "NO" from my apartment. One evening the enemy shot a fiery arrow. There I was in my fighting stance with my Shield of Faith, and a very quiet little "no" came out. Surprised, I was given the understanding that it is not the word "no" itself, but the power behind the word. Jesus is the Word. He is always in the battle; I never stand-alone.

I hope these lessons, with their tools and comforts will be of value to you: that the Word of God becomes the fire that warms you, the light in your cave, the filter of your mind, and the guard of your heart.

~ ~ ~ ~ ~

I spoke of not having a honeymoon at the start of my journey, but there were always the roses:

A dozen dark red roses, to remember Jesus's shed blood.

When the road traveled was hard, a single long stem rose.

A great disappointment, three yellow roses tied together with a beautiful satin ribbon.

Heartbreak, a fully opened white rose.

His love sent like roses to heal a relationship thought never to be mended.

The roses that glowed pink on the cheeks of my grandchildren as they were born into our family.

A pair of cardinals sent to sit on my porch railing, my heart sang with their flashing red color—like two red roses, their dewdrops sparkling in the sunshine.

Sadness and failure, roses fading, petals falling.

Guilt, a rose covered.

Forgiveness, a tightly closed rose bud … opens.

A squirrel sent to drive me a little crazy then to double me up with laughter, a "Circus rose."

A quiet mind, a "Peace rose."

The Prince of Peace, always near.

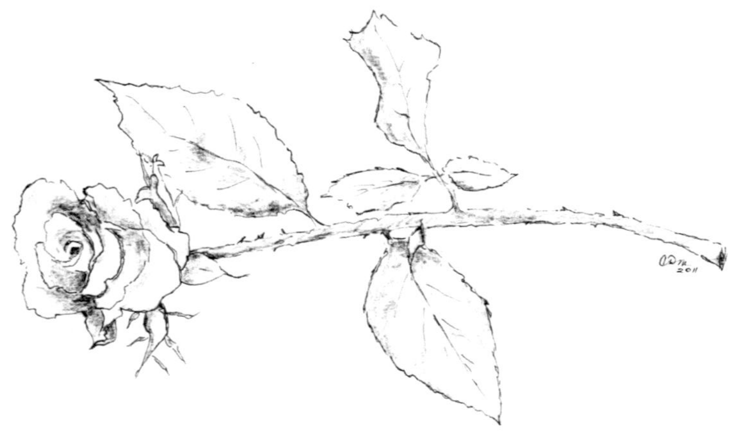

I earnestly pray this book blesses you a thousand times over.

"May we be as a pleasing fragrance to the heart of the Father, the Son and the Holy Spirit."

*In His Service, Charlene*

# About the Author

Charlene Mueller, mother of two, grandmother to six, is a past president of an Aglow International Lighthouse, serving ten years. She attends Maranatha Assembly of God Church in McHenry, Illinois. She has garnered a few nicknames over her life, including Sparkplug and Pit Bull, (a funny story for another time), but the one she lights up to is Encourager, as this is her heart.

*Email Charlene for availability of paintings:*

PaintingwithGod@muellernetwork.com

www.ingramcontent.com/pod-product-compliance
Lightning Source LLC
Chambersburg PA
CBRC091242050726
47599CB00009B/964